# Wake Up to Wonder

# Praise for *Wake Up to Wonder*

What a delight to read *Wake Up to Wonder*. Its uplifting tone and carefully crafted words quickly alter the reader's outlook from dismal to hope on steroids! Whitney's deep spiritual connection to the God of wonder emerges and inspires the expectation that desirable change is possible. Penetrating personal illustrations, Scriptural applications, and practical measures to follow awaken the joy of living and loving. I'm grateful for the opportunity to immerse myself in these elevating pages and believe that God is going to use them to gift His children with wonder. I heartily endorse *Wake Up to Wonder* and commend it to every searching mind and heart.

—**Marlene Chase**, author, former editor in chief and national literary secretary of the Salvation Army USA

Here is a drum roll in words for Whitney Hopler's book *Wake Up to Wonder*. Embracing the wonder around us is a precursor to everything good that God gives us: Opening our eyes to the marvels around us and taking our place in the 'wonder-ful' world. Whitney leads us on a pursuit of God's wonder, one step at a time. I know Whitney personally, and she is the quintessential woman full of wonder herself. It only takes a few minutes with her to catch her joyful vision of the world. This spills over into her writing and you will be blessed by her words.

—**Betsey Kodat**, author, Capital Christian Writers Fellowship prayer coordinator

This book is an unabashedly spiritual book—not a religious one. The author, Whitney Hopler, argues for awe, not adoration of a particular religious dogma. Braiding personal stories—some of which had me gasping in awe—with research in a deftly woven, well-written text, Whitney tells us why her story of prayer and meditation could be ours. Reading her soft and flowing prose slowed me down enough to look out the window at the trees blowing in a summer breeze and feel a renewed sense of wonder.

—**Steve Gladis**, PhD, executive team coach, leadership speaker, author, George Mason University's Center for the Advancement of Well-Being senior scholar

In the last decade, science has more fully embraced the notion of an afterlife. Compelling, verifiable accounts from physicians and their patients of near-death experiences reveal the magnificence of a dimension beyond our own. So now that we have thousands of credible reports of the heaven that awaits us, the next question is: How might we bring what we are learning of heaven to earth today? Whitney Hopler answers this question in her book *Wake to Up to Wonder.* Whitney invites us to live in a state of awe while we are on earth and, not only to live with the intellectual awareness that God and an afterlife exist, but to bring this knowledge into everything we do by living in wonder. In these challenging days, there is so much that can distract us from the beauty of this world and how everything is infused with the Divine. Whitney's book offers a lens for living in which all things are revealed in their beauty—so that we can experience in everyday life the magic of the world that exists beyond the threshold and celebrate that heaven is all around us.

—**Lisa Smartt**, author, *Words at the Threshold* and *Cante Bardo*

*Wake Up to Wonder* comes to us at a crucial moment in society as we're searching for deeper meaning and insights around the growing COVID-19 pandemic and racial injustices. Whitney Hopler brings the science of wonder and religious doctrine alive with her profound stories throughout this book. The book reaches beyond religion into the realm of spirituality and how awe-filled experiences connect us to higher purposes that go beyond ourselves. Her provocative questions inspire and challenge us to think more deeply about concepts such as pursuing wonder, discovering awe through love, and turning away from our fears and toward our faith. Awe has the power to lift our perspective beyond our problems to where we can see how profoundly we're all connected in a wondrous human family, where we're meant to thrive together.

—**Nance Lucas**, PhD, executive director and chief well-being officer, George Mason University's Center for the Advancement of Well-Being

My parents taught my siblings and me to cultivate lifelong learning, which opened for us a gateway to curiosity, wonder, and a hunger for creative pursuits. *Wake Up to Wonder* taps into that process with key biblical components to finding contentment and joy in the simple, beautiful gifts God has placed all around us. It is possible never to experience a day of boredom in your life. Fulfillment and purpose are attainable, and *Wake Up to Wonder* shows us the path to reaching those goals.

—**Mary Fairchild**, author, editor, *Stories of Calvary,* LearnReligions.com, GotQuestions.org, RevelintheRubble. com

*Wake Up to Wonder* is an eloquent guide full of important insights for those of us who long for more beauty and meaning to enter our lives. The vivid stories in *Wake up to Wonder* work as important reminders for how to experience a life filled with more awe, peace, and faith. Whitney Hopler has written a must-read book for anyone longing for more direct spiritual experiences in their lives, and the tips about the importance of meditation, prayer, and letting go of fear are timely.

—**Tricia Barker**, author, *Angels in the OR*

Whitney Hopler is an excellent author as evidenced by all her contributions to the study of well-being through her writing. Awe is an integral part of a person's holistic wellness, and Whitney does a great job of conveying the importance of awe in her book, *Wake Up to Wonder.* While this book has a Christian perspective, I believe the content of this book is universal to all people who are looking to increase their happiness. I highly recommend this book to anyone who finds the study of happiness and well-being fascinating.

—**Philip Wilkerson**, "Positive Philter" podcast host, George Mason University's well-being university committee member

Too often, we sleepwalk through our real life, focusing on the next item on our to-do list, the next promotion, the next new vehicle or home or electronic must-have. That's no way to live. Whitney Hopler gently encourages us to open ourselves up to the wonders God desires to share with us ... if only we will slow down long enough to let that happen. Take a break with God and Whitney—you will be the better for it.

—**Melanie Rigney**, author, editor, RejoiceBeGlad. com

Whitney Hopler's book *Wake up to Wonder* offers readers an opportunity to recognize the daily power of God's grace. When we take time to fill our lives with prayer, worship, and practices to thrive in the Spirit, our lives can be better.

—**Lewis Forrest II**, MEd, higher education professional, and well-being advocate

Many of us walk through life with our heads down and our eyes fixed on the ground. But that's not how God created us to be. We're to enjoy his creation, to marvel at all he has given us. Whitney Hopler's *Wake Up to Wonder* shows us how we can all benefit from reconnecting with the wonders of God.

—**Sarah Hamaker**, parent coach, author, Capital Christian Writers Fellowship president

Whitney Hopler has a passion and graceful nature to spread joy, hope, and awe around this world. Through a faithful approach to examine the wonder in your everyday life, reading Hopler's words will inspire you to live life to its fullest and appreciate the journey God placed you on.

—**Christie Michals**, George Mason University's well-being university committee member

Whitney Hopler's intriguing book, *Wake Up to Wonder*, reminded me of an experience from my childhood. While taking a walk through a pine forest one afternoon, I found myself completely enveloped in God's loving presence. In response, my young heart overflowed with praise. I had never named this encounter until I read Whitney's book. The author tells of her own experiences with God through nature, her senses, the gifts of the Spirit, books and learning, worship, prayer, and meditation, etc.—wonders God wants us to see, feel and enjoy. Each chapter takes the reader deeper into a richer relationship with God. As Whitney says, "Wonder shows you more about God and inspires you to move closer to him." Prepare to be challenged—you'll never view another sunset without being awakened to the awe and wonder of an amazing God.

—**Claudette Renalds**, author, *By the Sea, Journey to Hope.*

# Wake Up to Wonder

## Whitney Hopler

PUBLISHING THE POSITIVE

ELK LAKE PUBLISHING INC
Plymouth, Massachusetts

Cover and Interior Design: Derinda Babcock

Editor(s): Peggy Ellis, Susan K. Stewart, Deb Haggerty

PUBLISHED BY: Elk Lake Publishing, Inc., 35 Dogwood Drive, Plymouth, MA 02360, 2020

---

Library Cataloging Data

Names: Hopler, Whitney (Whitney Hopler)

*Wake Up to Wonder* / Hopler, Whitney

p. 23cm × 15cm (9in × 6 in.)

Identifiers: ISBN-13: 978-1-64949-015-5 (paperback) | 978-1-64949-016-2 (trade paperback) | 978-1-64949-017-9 (e-book)

Key Words: awe, inspirational, spiritual growth, healthy spirituality, miracles, God, Jesus

LCCN: 2020946591 Nonfiction

## Dedication

I dedicate this book to my daughter, Honor, and my son, Justin. Thank you both for being such wonderful people.

# Table of Contents

# Acknowledgments

Thanks to God, the source of all wonder, for calling me to write this book and providing everything I needed to do so. I am constantly in awe of you.

Thanks to everyone who has ever encouraged me to write. I'm grateful to a team of people too numerous to mention. Special thanks to my father, Jim Wyckoff, who taught me the wonder of words through newspapers and has enthusiastically cheered me on to write through the years.

Thanks to my friends and fellow writers from Capital Christian Writers Fellowship who commented on drafts and supported this book in prayer. Thanks to my husband, Russ, for your caring support for this book.

Thanks to the talented team at Elk Lake Publishing, Inc. (especially Deb Haggerty, Peggy Ellis, Susan Stewart, and Derinda Babcock) for your valuable contributions to this book.

# Introduction

The Milky Way galaxy glittered overhead as my family and I drove back to our Oregon cabin near Crater Lake National Park. We pulled over to the side of the road, so we could walk out into the deep darkness and stare at the galaxy's lights overhead. This was much more than the smattering of white dots visible when stargazing at home in Virginia. There was a riot of color—green, purple, pink, and orange—streaking across more white dots than I could count. The celestial display looked like someone in space had knocked over a jewelry box, spilling out a multitude of pearly stars and colorful necklaces of light. Seeing our planet's home galaxy in person opened a window to wonder. Through that window, I could see how I was an active part of God's great design. I felt tiny, yet significant, while staring upward. My family and I stood there in silence for several minutes, absorbing the pure splendor of the sky. We only looked away when loud snorting sounds alerted us to cattle nearby. We were near a ranch, but due to the pitch black of the night, we could not see the cattle snorting at us. Laughing, we reluctantly got back into our car to continue driving. Our view had shrunk back down to earth, but our souls were enriched by the wonder we had just seen.

When we see something as overwhelmingly wonderful as the Milky Way, we're compelled to pay attention. Too often, however, we miss out on the wonder all around us.

That happens when we're focused on surviving rather than thriving. We rush through our to-do lists, struggle with our worries, and tell ourselves wonder is a luxury. Consumed by stress or fear, our souls become desensitized to the everyday miracles happening in our lives. Wonder seems too impractical to enjoy on a regular basis. We seem to be going through life asleep and unaware of what matters most. Yet our craving for wonder never leaves us. Whenever we search the night sky for stars, we're looking for wonder. God—the ultimate source of wonder—has created us with that craving. We are wired to notice and enjoy wonder on a regular basis, because wonder connects us with our Creator—the God who "performs wonders that cannot be fathomed, miracles that cannot be counted" (Job 5:9).

We all know how experiencing wonder feels in our souls. A feeling of awe overwhelms us, delighted surprise fuels our curiosity, and astonishment inspires us to thank God for our blessings.

Wonder can show up in our lives from extraordinary life events, such as falling in love with someone, accomplishing a major goal at work, or celebrating a miraculous answer to prayer. However, we don't need to experience something dramatic to experience awe. We can encounter wonder through simple pursuits like hiking in a park, listening to music, or eating a meal. An ordinary experience can give us an extraordinary glimpse of God at work in our lives. By simply paying attention, we can wake up to the wonder of something holy that reminds us of God's presence with us.

Experiencing wonder on a regular basis is essential to living well. Research shows there many powerful well-being benefits of wonder, from less stress to more happiness. In my work at George Mason University's

Center for the Advancement of Well-Being, I regularly see how the latest well-being research is helping people live in ways that help them fulfill their God-given purposes. I'll describe research into wonder and well-being throughout this book. An overview of academic research into awe (a synonym for wonder) by the Greater Good Science Center at the University of California, Berkeley[1] provides a quick overview of why wonder is so important to us.

That review of awe research by many different institutions shows experiencing awe is associated with a myriad of well-being benefits. Those benefits include *more* life satisfaction, positive emotions (such as happiness, peace, and gratitude), spiritual feelings, interest in learning, humility, kindness, generosity, and connection to others. Those benefits also include *less* stress, materialism, anxiety, and levels of physical inflammation linked to many diseases.

God designed you, me, and every person on this planet to enjoy wonderful lives. We can—and should—give ourselves permission to, at any age, experience wonder as children do. "Truly I tell you, unless you change and become like little children, you will never enter the kingdom of heaven," Jesus Christ reveals in Matthew 18:3. We adults can learn a lot from the curious minds and open hearts that help children experience wonder. Children, who are souls fresh from heaven, naturally pursue awe because they feel the craving for wonder God has placed in all of us. As adults, we tend to become desensitized as we're exposed to pain over the years and numb ourselves to cope with our anguish. After a while, we can lose our ability to notice and appreciate the awe around us. The good news is we can always wake up our souls to wonder.

During our journey together, I'll give you lots of practical steps you can use to develop a lifestyle of regularly enjoying wonder. You may know me already from the thousands of popular articles I've written about faith for places such as Crosswalk.com, Dotdash.com, and the Salvation Army's national magazines. Yet while you may know my work, you may not realize I was a workaholic for many years. Being an overachiever, plus a bad habit of worrying, caused me to miss wonder every day. Countless experiences of awe passed me by because I was afraid pursuing wonder would somehow be irresponsible or impractical.

A crisis shook me out of the habits that blocked wonder in my life. My husband Russ, who had seemed healthy, suddenly struggled with kidney disease. Without a transplant, his life was soon in danger. While we frantically searched for a kidney donor, I prayed I wouldn't become a widowed single mother of two young children. Thankfully, through a series of events only God could have orchestrated, a heroic man from our church donated the kidney Russ needed.

God's love worked so powerfully through our experience, I decided never to live another day without fully appreciating that awe is a wondrous gift from God. I wanted to open the gift of each new day and enjoy its wonders in every way possible. My old fear-based habits couldn't continue for my desire to become reality, so I started on a journey toward wonder that has revolutionized my life.

You can take the same journey in your life. As we walk through this book together, you'll read about my love for God, the source of all wonder. You'll notice this book is written from a Christian perspective. That's because my relationship with Jesus is a vital part of how I have experienced awe. I believe Jesus truly is who he claimed to be (one member of the Holy Trinity). I also believe God's love extends to all people, and he meets all of us wherever we are. Regardless of what beliefs (or lack of beliefs) you have, God offers you the privilege of opening the gift of awe in your life. No matter what your spiritual journey looks like, you can move closer to wonder through this book.

On the journey through these pages, you'll discover, enjoy, and learn from awe. You can enjoy a wonderful life in any circumstances. No matter how busy you are, no matter what you can afford, no matter how many problems you have, you can still experience awe regularly.

There's no lack of wonder to experience in our world, once we recognize this gift. Let's ask God to "open my eyes that I may see wonderful things" (Psalm 119:18) together.

Renowned physicist Albert Einstein said, "There are only two ways to live your life. One is as though nothing is a miracle. The other is as though everything is a miracle."[2] Through this book, we can start to experience the miracle of wonder in everything. Wonder is waiting for us. Let's get this party started.

# Chapter 1

# Connect with God through Prayer and Meditation

From a hilltop in Israel's Golan Heights, I could see into Syria. The thought of the civil war raging there—and the tremendous pain the Syrian people were suffering—moved me to walk away from our tour group and sit on a rock at the edge of a parking lot to pray. I closed my eyes and prayed that God's peace, compassion, and mercy would still somehow be able to reach the individual Syrians caught up in tragic human conflict. As I prayed silently, through my thoughts, I expressed the grief and helplessness I felt from news reports about the men, women, and children harmed or killed in the war. I poured my heart out to God about how overwhelming the situation was for people who lived so close to where I was praying, yet were separated from me by vastly different circumstances. There I sat as a tourist with the freedom and resources to travel on a pilgrimage, while they were trapped in a desperate situation.

I finished praying and opened my eyes. A white horse stood in front of me. The tall and muscular animal appeared to be extraordinarily powerful yet looked down at me with gentle brown eyes. Startled but not afraid, I stared back at the horse, and the more I gazed into his eyes the more I felt a sense of love and peace, despite the anguish I had felt when praying. I felt even more than that.

Somehow, I felt like the horse had heard and understood my silent yet fervent prayer. How was that possible?

Thoughts came to me as the horse and I looked at each other. *God loves every soul in Syria completely. God's heart breaks over the war there. God wants all people to have compassion on each other. God's permissive will allows war to happen, perhaps to allow good to win over evil.*

Finally, I broke my gaze and looked around the parking lot and the surrounding area. There were no other horses. Since horses usually travel in herds, it was unlikely the horse walked there by himself. There were no horse trailers in the lot, and no one else was watching the horse. I didn't see how the horse could have been transported there, either. I looked back at the wonderful creature and saw he was still gazing at me. "Hello," I said, slowing rising from my seat on the rock. He took a few steps back to give me space—all while continuing to look straight at me. I wanted to reach out to pet the horse's flowing white mane, but before I could extend a hand, he backed away a bit more.

I bent down to pick up my water bottle from beside the rock, intending to walk back to the tour group and point the horse out to others. When I looked up a few seconds later, though, the horse was gone. There was no trace of him anywhere for as far as I could see in any direction. The horse had simply disappeared. After I described him to everyone back on the bus, I learned no one else in our group had seen the horse. Why had no one else noticed such a large creature standing in the parking lot? He had been so majestic and had made such a strong impression on me. In fact, I couldn't shake the sense that, somehow, I had been in the presence of something holy.

What, or who, was that magnificent horse? Was he a flesh-and-blood animal God communicated through? Was he an angel manifesting in that way? Was he a visitation from God's Spirit in a physical form? I don't know. Reflecting on the encounter later, I thought of the biblical passage in Revelation 19 that describes Jesus Christ and his heavenly army riding on white horses. In every faith tradition, a white horse symbolizes the purity that comes from holiness.

Although I can't explain why I had that experience, I'm sure my heartfelt prayer led to it.

Prayer and meditation can lead us to awe in powerful ways. Communicating with our Creator is an awesome privilege. But it's so readily available to us, we can take that privilege for granted. We can also get so busy and distracted we start to view prayer and meditation as obligations rather than opportunities. Neglecting prayer and meditation is easy if we don't connect those spiritual disciplines to wonder.

Prayer is talking, while meditation is listening. We don't need to complicate processes God has designed to be simple. But we also shouldn't discount the significant ways prayer and meditation can help us discover wonder.

Research from neuroscientist Andrew Newberg shows how prayer and meditation can change our brains.[1] When people pray or meditate, key areas in their brains become activated. Praying and meditating both activate the frontal lobes (the brain's area for paying attention and concentrating), which is vital for noticing and appreciating wonder. In addition, praying activates the inferior parietal lobe (the brain's language area).

Another study divided Christian participants into two groups with different assignments: they were either to engage in meditative prayer on Bible passages or they were to listen to lectures on the Gospels. The group of people who focused on meditative prayer reported more experiences of awe than the group who just listened to lectures.[2] Other research has found experiencing wonder as a result of prayer promotes faith in God and the supernatural in general, and increases the likelihood people interpret events as having God-given purposes.[3]

## ESCAPE FROM NOISE

After my family and I drove into the National Radio Quiet Zone (a 13,000-square-mile area around the National Radio Astronomy Observatory in Green Bank, West Virginia), the noise level in our car suddenly dropped dramatically. The radio no longer got reception, so we turned it off. Our cell phones no longer received signals, so we stopped using them. A beautiful landscape of woods and hills lined both sides of the road. We gazed out our windows and were content not to talk while we soaked in the view. When we arrived to tour the observatory—home of the world's largest moving telescope—we were in the center of the quiet zone. The equipment measures radio waves traveling to Earth from objects in space, such as planets, comets, galaxies, and quasars. Astronomers from all over the world use the data to learn more about what's happening in space, from areas nearby our planet to locations billions of light years away. Some of the experiments even delve into the search for extraterrestrial life. Quiet is essential to the observatory's work, since electromagnetic noise could interfere with the radio signals the telescopes are discovering and recording. By blocking out noise, observatory scientists notice and learn from signals the universe is sending out.

God is always broadcasting in our direction. Noise, however, often distracts us from tuning into the wonder of what God wants us to discover. We're inundated with noise every day. Our alarms beep to wake us. Our mobile devices buzz to notify us of calls, texts, and emails. Our family, friends, and coworkers talk to us—if they can get our attention away from work, entertainment, advertising, and social media, which competes with them to be heard. Even our own thoughts can be a cacophony of information loudly shouting at us. Wonder is all around us, waiting for us to notice. However, wonder often speaks in quiet ways that require us to listen carefully. To hear the wondrous messages God sends us, we need to take breaks from the noise of our busy day-to-day lives.

That's why including quiet prayer and meditation times in our schedules is necessary. We can plan these quiet times whenever and however they work best—daytime, nighttime, at home, or out and about. But we can't afford to skip them, or we simply won't be able to hear the inspiring sounds of wonder well.

## BREAK FREE FROM FORMULAS

Glancing at the Bible, notebook, and pen I usually used for my morning devotional time, I felt a wave of guilt wash over me. This morning, I had an early appointment for work, so I didn't have time to fit my regular routine into my schedule. That routine had grown to nearly an hour. I incorporated all sorts of formulas into my devotional time, trying a little bit of various ways to pray and meditate I'd either read about or that someone I knew had personally recommended. Prayer formulas I used included the Lord's Prayer (the example Jesus gave of how to pray), the ACTS prayer method (adoration, confession, thanksgiving, and supplication), Lectio Divina (reading Scripture in conversation with God), and breath prayer (praying phrases that can be said in one breath). Mindfulness meditation formulas I used included breath awareness meditation (paying attention to breathing to focus), centering meditation (focusing on God as the center of life and, in turn, receiving peace from God), and loving kindness meditation (sending love out into the world).

Between following all the formulas and taking notes, I had developed a daily routine that was sometimes overwhelming. Yet, in my zeal to connect more deeply with God, I dared not neglect all those different ways which were supposed to work. This morning, however, I simply didn't have time.

Passing by my devotional corner, I rushed out the door and began driving to my appointment. "I'm sorry, God," I said aloud in the privacy of my car. But even as those words left my mouth, I didn't truly feel I meant them. I was relieved to take a break from my routine, which had begun to seem as much of an obligation as the work appointment to which I was driving. Free of the formulas I had imposed on myself, I simply used my commute to talk to God as if he was sitting right beside me in the car. Even though I couldn't see him strapping on a seatbelt and looking over at me, I knew his Spirit was with me anywhere and anytime. My prayers poured out naturally, even though I didn't use a single formula to express them. Then, a few minutes before I arrived at my appointment, I stopped talking, asked God to speak to me, and simply listened. A steady flow of guidance, inspiration, and love came into my mind and heart. The wonder of this pure, unforced communication with God carried me into my workday with more joy than I'd experienced in a long time.

The next morning, I let go of all my formulaic prayer and meditation methods and simply enjoyed praying and meditating naturally. In the years since then, I've expanded my perspective on what counts as prayer and meditation. *We're praying and meditating in any way we choose to focus our energy on talking with, and listening to, God.* There's no problem if we don't speak holy-sounding words out loud when we pray. We don't have to worry if we can't sit still or be quiet in meditation. We can write our prayers, dance our prayers, or simply think them silently. We can meditate while doing housework, cooking a meal, or walking around our neighborhoods.

In Isaiah 29, God becomes frustrated with the people's formulaic communication with him and decides to reach out to them with wonder to engage their hearts. God declares: "Therefore once more I will astound these people with wonder upon wonder; the wisdom of the wise will perish, the intelligence of the intelligent will vanish" (v. 14). We can—and should—smile, laugh, cry, shout, etc. during prayer and meditation whenever we feel moved to do so. Praying and meditating honestly from our hearts, instead of following formulas, can help us experience the wonder of God reaching out to us from his heart.

God has no barriers to loving communication, so we shouldn't have any either. When we break free from formulas, we can stop seeing prayer and meditation as chores and start enjoying the pure wonder of communicating with God. Then, once we've rediscovered that wonder, we can use a formula if that's helpful for a specific purpose. For example, sometimes I say the Lord's Prayer before I pray anything else, because I've found the words open my mind and heart to help me perceive and receive God's messages well. I don't often pray in structured ways anymore. I pray throughout each day and night, in response to what I'm thinking about at the time. I maintain a close connection to God, but in a way I enjoy. I love to talk and listen to God in conversational ways. This works best for me.

On a day-to-day basis, we can feel free to pray and meditate however we like. We can trust God to meet us through any form of communication.

## LET GO OF AGENDAS

As I sat down in our church's sanctuary, I glanced dejectedly at the empty seat beside me, where I had hoped my mom would be sitting. She had turned me down yet again after I had invited her to church. Sighing, I said a prayer asking God to convince Mom to join a church—either mine, or one closer to her home. I had been praying that same agenda for many years. So far, I saw no progress happening, but I was determined to keep asking. I was praying for something positive that would please God and bless Mom. God eventually *had* to answer and somehow convince Mom to participate in a church congregation, I rationalized. Someone I hadn't met before sat down next to me. I smiled at her even as tears welled up in my eyes. How long would it take for Mom to come to church? Would she *ever* do so? Over the years I had prayed for Mom, she had gradually moved from atheist to agnostic to a seeker who was genuinely interested in God. God was clearly at work in her life, but her persistent refusal to go to church baffled and grieved me. Without being a part of a community of believers, she was missing out on so much that could help her grow closer to God.

The pulsing beat of a worship song lifted my spirit, and I stood up to sing along. Opening my hands and raising them into the air, I symbolically gave the situation to God. I knew God wouldn't interfere with Mom's free will, yet I believed he would keep inspiring her to grow closer to him. *How* that would all unfold was a mystery to me.

I wish I could say I let go of my agenda after that day. However, for a few more years, I kept praying for Mom to join a church—and kept getting disappointed and discouraged when she didn't.

Then one night, God sent Mom a life-changing encounter with wonder.

By this time, she was fighting leukemia in a hospital. During one of my visits, Mom told me she had seen an angel outside her window the previous night. In an awestruck voice, Mom reported the angel gestured her hands, sending several mysterious objects which looked like golden ovals through the window and into Mom's chest. After that encounter, medical tests revealed healing in Mom's body—the cancer went into remission and her pneumonia cleared up. However, the healing in Mom's soul was the most profound gift.

After God sent one of his heavenly messengers to her, Mom finally put her faith enthusiastically in God. She grew close to him until she passed away two months later from an infection. Through that encounter with wonder, God inspired Mom in a way that gave her enough time to place her trust in him. Mom never joined a church in those last months, so the agenda I'd prayed about for twenty-three years never happened. However, God's answer to my prayers was more wonderful than what I could have expected. God didn't fulfill my agenda, but instead accomplished a greater goal: Mom's salvation.

Our prayers are powerful. God will *always* answer them, but the answers he chooses may blow our agendas out of the water. Ephesians 3:20 reminds us God "is able to do immeasurably more than all we ask or imagine, according to his power that is at work within us." We may think we know what's best for a person or situation, but the truth is our human perspectives are quite limited compared to that of our omniscient God. If we pray only for our own agendas, we limit the possibilities God can see and potentially block the wonder of how God really wants to answer. By letting go of agendas when we pray, we can welcome wonder in any way God wants to send it to us.

## COMMUNICATE WITH GOD ANYTIME AND ANYWHERE

Sitting in the dentist's office waiting for my children to finish getting their teeth cleaned, I decided to use the downtime to meditate. I closed my eyes in the middle of the crowded waiting room and quieted my mind. After a brief time of meditation, a vivid image of my husband Russ came to me. He was struggling underwater in what looked like an ocean, fighting to reach the surface and breathe. A strong voice shouted in my mind. *Pray for Russ! He's in danger right now.*

The mental image I saw didn't make any sense to me. As far as I knew, Russ was inside a hotel conference room that day, meeting with people at business conference in Mexico. Yet the image of him underwater was clear, and the urge to pray was too strong to ignore. So, surrounded by the droning noise of dental equipment, I prayed fervently yet silently for God to help Russ with whatever dangerous situation he was facing. After a few minutes, a feeling of peace washed over me.

On the phone later that day, Russ told me that at the exact time I had prayed for him—precisely to the minute when we calculated the time zone differences—he had been in danger of drowning. Russ and a coworker had fallen into the ocean during a team-building event, and the panicked coworker had grabbed onto him so hard she pulled both of them down into the deep. Russ fought hard to stop them from sinking, but the struggle was too difficult, and soon he couldn't breathe anymore. Just as Russ realized there was nothing more he could do, he got a sudden surge of energy that empowered him to reach the water's surface and pull the coworker to safety. God had answered my prayer from the dentist's office far away in Virginia, saving Russ and his colleague from drowning.

We can experience wonder anytime and anywhere— even in the most mundane situations—if we maintain regular communication with God. Praying and meditating can connect us to wonder every time we put them into action. Sometimes, God will simply give us the awe-inspiring gifts of peace or encouragement. At other times, God will work through us to do something extraordinary. We never know what type of wonder we can encounter through prayer or meditation. Yet we can always expect to discover wonder by communicating with God.

## MAKE A PILGRIMAGE

Stepping onto the island of Mont St. Michel, I literally jumped for joy that I was there. The iconic French destination known as *La Merveille* (The Wonder), rising dramatically on a rock in the middle of a bay, has long been a destination for spiritual pilgrimages. People have been visiting the island (originally called Mont Tombe) to pray since ancient times. Archangel Michael appeared to a bishop named Aubert in the year 708 AD, the bishop reported, asking that a church be built there to honor God and encourage more people to visit on pilgrimage. Soon after, Mont St. Michel became one of the world's most popular sites for spiritual pilgrims.

Everything about Mont St. Michel's natural features called out to my soul with wonder when I began exploring the island: the pyramid-shaped granulite crystalline rock, the water rushing in and out of the bay with the fast tides, and the wind blowing powerfully. As I walked up the steep path, through the village and toward the abbey, I joined a huge crowd of my fellow visitors. We walked together in a great mass of humanity. Although most of the people around me were strangers, I felt connected to them by our mutual pursuit of awe. Glancing at the bay at various points along the path, I noticed a new perspective each time. Then I reached the top. When I looked out from the summit, the sky and water seemed to blend together, the breeze carried the pungent scent of salt mixed with the sweet aroma of flowers, and a seagull landed with youthful vigor on an ancient rock wall. The wondrous balance of God's creation was on full display.

Gratefully, I spent the day and evening on Mont St. Michel, exploring its history on a tour, visiting its museums, watching its storied tides rush in and out, and celebrating its creative inspiration at a light and sound show. But the greatest wonder happened when I simply prayed and meditated in the abbey's church. No profound new insights came to me. Yet, I still experienced something profound. I felt God's presence, which I knew by faith was always with me, but which I was sometimes prone to forget. Being in a pilgrimage place sparked wonder in my soul, helping me notice and remember what matters most. God says to all of us: "You will seek me and find me when you seek me with all your heart" (Jeremiah 29:13).

A pilgrimage to a specific place where we seek God wholeheartedly reminds us what a privilege we have to be able to communicate with our Creator. Afterward, when we return to our everyday lives, we can reflect on the awe we experienced on pilgrimage and be motivated to keep pursing wonder through prayer and meditation.

## SEE PRAYER AND MEDITATION AS OPPORTUNITIES TO ENCOUNTER WONDER

We'll no longer see prayer and meditation as obligations when we expect to experience God's love through those practices. Instead, we'll see praying and meditating are powerful opportunities to encounter wonder.

Job 37:14 encourages us to "stop and consider God's wonders." We need to reflect on God's awesome power and wondrous works to gain a greater perspective on life, just as Job did. Prayer and meditation are the tools we can use to do so. Research shows that both praying[4] and meditating[5] can open people's minds to think more creatively, leading them to discover wonder as a result.

Give prayer and meditation a try as often as you can. Start expecting to encounter God in wonderful ways whenever you pray or meditate. You won't be disappointed.

## QUESTIONS TO PONDER FOR WONDER

1. What challenges do you need to overcome to start praying and meditating more? Are they attitudes (such as feeling pressure to follow formulas) or lifestyle issues (such as getting distracted by the noise of life's stresses)?
2. How can you let go right now of one agenda that you've been praying about, to stop limiting the wonder of how God may choose to surprise you?
3. When and how can you incorporate prayer and meditation into your busy schedule on the go?

4. Where are a few ordinary places you'd like to try praying or meditating?

5. Where would you like to go on a spiritual pilgrimage in search of wonder? How can you start planning now to make the trip?

# Chapter 2

## Manage Stress Well

Thoughts of all the chores and errands my family and I needed to do swirled around my mind as we walked through a local botanical garden. After a busy week at work and school, we had spontaneously decided to let our long to-do list of cleaning, shopping, etc., wait so we could enjoy some weekend fun together instead. Yet, the stress of all we had to do nagged me. I took a path toward a cluster of rose bushes and decided to literally "stop and smell the roses." As I leaned over a yellow rose and inhaled, a sweet scent seemed to permeate my whole being with wonder. Delighted, I sniffed the fragrances of every rose bush variety there. Inhaling each aroma felt like inhaling God's grace—a gift of wonder he gave me unconditionally. I didn't have to complete any chores or errands to earn this awesome experience. God offered the privilege to me anytime I chose to enjoy it. Exhaling in between sniffing the roses felt like I was letting go of more and more stress each time.

I encountered awe with every step throughout the rest of the garden. Everything there—from the tallest trees to the shortest blades of grass—relied on the wondrous system God had designed to sustain them. Sunlight, water, and soil nourished the plants day by day. I recalled what Jesus said about the "lilies of the field" who "toil not, neither do they spin" (Matthew 6:28) and yet God cares for them so they don't need to be stressed.

We purchased a few items to take home from the garden shop, including a bouquet of mixed summer flowers and tomatoes on vines. Whenever I looked at those flowers, wonder reminded me not to worry about my to-do list, but simply to do what I could, with gratitude for God's grace and peace. When I plucked the tomatoes off their vines to put them in our salads, awe reminded me of Jesus's words in John 15:5: "I am the vine; you are the branches. If you remain in me and I in you, you will bear much fruit; apart from me you can do nothing." There was no need to stress out about chores, errands, or anything else as long as I stayed connected to God.

## WAYS WE NUMB OURSELVES

A paramedic I met at a children's birthday talked about regularly giving himself IV fluids to recover from a hangover. "I've figured out exactly how to numb myself to achieve the maximum buzz with the minimum risk," he told a group of us parents in between sips of beer. "You wouldn't believe how drunk I can get without a hangover. Ever since I lost custody of my kids in the divorce, I've been working on my buzz—and now, I'm feeling no pain." He laughed with a tremulous tone that told me he was sadder than he seemed to be.

Even though the paramedic seemed proud he had come up with a plan to drink his feelings into oblivion, I couldn't help but think how much better life would be for him to face his pain in a sober state. That would be challenging and possibly even excruciating at first. Ultimately, however, facing the pain would lead him to the wonder of noticing how God was at work amid his pain. As a paramedic, he was used to helping patients heal from painful situations. By planning regular drinking binges to try to numb the pain in his life, though, he was blocking his own healing process.

Too often, we numb ourselves in ways that deaden our senses, block our ability to feel our emotions, and prevent us from noticing the wonder that is happening all around us. Those ways include everything from bad habits like constant busyness, overeating, shopping too much, and watching excessive TV to addictions such as pornography, alcohol, or gambling. God has wired us to feel our emotions—including difficult feelings such as sadness, anger, and loneliness—so we can learn important lessons from working through them.

The temptation to rely on something else that's emotionally numbing is still common in our society. Here are five of the most common numbing strategies.

1. **Comforting activities:** We may block uncomfortable feelings through a variety of activities that make us feel temporarily safe—eating a comfort food (such as pizza or ice cream), shopping for something that we don't need, biting our nails, or doing anything else that feels comforting. Food is especially popular. Research from the American Psychological Association[1] shows that 38 percent of US adults say they have overeaten or eaten unhealthy foods in the past month because of stress.

2. **Screen time:** We may distract ourselves from our feelings by spending too much time watching screens—binge watching television, playing hours of video games, or mindlessly surfing online. People spend huge amounts of time each day staring at

screens. American adults average about eleven hours of daily screen time—most of their waking hours—a report from media company Nielson[2] reveals. The World Health Organization says that "excessive use" of screens is now a serious worldwide problem.[3]

3. **Busyness:** We may keep ourselves busy to push away challenging emotions we don't want to make time to feel. We can divert our attention to nearly any kind of work (paid or volunteer), which makes us feel good, or even fill our schedule with chores and errands to avoid focusing on difficult emotions. About 30 percent of Americans identify as workaholics, and about 86 percent of US males and about 66 percent of US females work more than full-time hours (forty hours) every week.[4]

4. **Pornography:** We may seek sexual arousal by viewing pornography, a cheap substitute for the wonder that can only come through intimacy as God designed it. The amount of people worldwide who view porn is staggering. In 2019, the world's largest porn website, Porn Hub, reported approximately forty-two *billion* visits to its site.[5] That's just one of many online porn sites. Even though porn destroys relationships, treats people who God loves as objects, and leads to dangerous addiction, 43 percent of Americans now believe that porn is morally acceptable, according to a Gallup poll.[6]

5. **Alcohol and other drugs:** We may numb our bodies with substances like alcoholic drinks and other types of drugs to try to escape emotions we don't want to feel. Substance abuse and addiction is prevalent in many nations around the world.

Worldwide, about 283 million people suffer from alcohol usage disorders and about thirty-one million people struggle with drug usage disorders (such as addiction to the powerful opioid pain killers, which have caused a worldwide crisis), according to reports from the World Health Organization.[7]

Numbing ourselves in ways like these can temporarily soothe the stress of feeling our challenging emotions. The more we try to escape our feelings through numbing methods, the more we put our souls to sleep. This severely limits the amount of wonder we can notice and enjoy. The way I've numbed myself most often is through busyness. As a recovering workaholic, I cringe to think about how much wonder I missed by keeping myself constantly busy with activities rather than making enough time for reflection.

How are you trying to relieve stress in your own life? Do you choose practices that connect you with God—the source of all wonder—to find peace when you're stressed? Or do you choose ways that numb you temporarily to stress but leave you feeling worse once the numbness wears off? Here's how to break free of numbing behaviors and replace them with healthy practices that connect you with God and wonder when you feel stressed.

1. **Start with prayer.** Confess the current ways you numb yourself for stress relief. Ask God to heal you from unhealthy cravings and free you from any addictions that stress triggers in you. Commit to stopping numbing behaviors for one month (changing a habit usually takes at least three weeks). Pray for help to change by replacing numbing behaviors with healthy practices when stress triggers your temptation to numb yourself.

2. **Cut ties to numbing behaviors you want to stop.** Make whatever lifestyle changes you can to cut your ties to unhealthy numbing behaviors during the month you've committed to stop them. For instance, if you've decided to stop eating certain unhealthy foods for comfort when you're stressed, throw out those foods you have at home and refuse to buy any more at the grocery store or at restaurants.

3. **Get support, encouragement, and accountability from others.** Find some trustworthy people who care about you and ask them to help you keep your commitment to change. Talk regularly with your circle of supporters and contact them whenever stress triggers urges for you to numb yourself. If you even suspect you may be dealing with an addiction to a numbing behavior, get professional counseling and other professional help—such as help from doctors, nurses, and rehab staff—to break your addiction.

4. **Replace numbing behaviors with mindful behaviors when you feel stressed.** Practice mindfulness when you feel the urge to numb yourself against stress. Mindfulness (focusing your awareness on the present moment, while calmly acknowledging and accepting your thoughts and feelings) can help you experience your emotions without being controlled by them. Mindfulness practices can be as simple as focusing on your breathing. Find ways to be mindful that help you relieve stress well, so you'll have specific practices to use in the moment whenever stressful feelings hit.

5. **Learn lessons God wants to teach you through your emotions.** God often uses emotions as teaching tools. Emotions are gifts from God, whom the Bible describes as having an emotional essence (1 John 4:8 declares "God is love."). Emotions constantly change as circumstances change. You may misinterpret emotions when you're not thinking of them from a Spirit-led perspective. Pray for guidance every day, asking God to help you discern the messages he sends you through your feelings. Rather than just reacting to your emotions, respond to them with the purpose of learning and growing closer to God in the process.

Really living like we believe God loves us and wants the best for us will give us emotional stability. When we get excited about the awe we can find in a close relationship with God, we can let go of cheap substitutes for God's love. The less we numb ourselves, the more sensitive we can become to wonder.

## PUT OUR EMOTIONS INTO MOTION

Tears flowed out of my son Justin's hazel eyes as he told me one of his preschool buddies was moving to another state, and he'd never get to play with his friend again. "It'll be okay," I said as I reached out to wipe away his tears. "You have plenty of other friends." Justin shook his head solemnly and backed away from my hands before I could dry his tears. "No, Mommy, don't," he said. "I *need* my tears."

His comment stopped me. What good were tears? I saw them only as unfortunate reminders of pain—something to numb myself against—as I grieved my mother's death. I hadn't allowed myself to cry a single tear since she'd passed away several years before. As I watched Justin continue to cry, I wondered if tears might be more than just something to brush away. Tears are a natural response to the pain we encounter in our fallen world. Crying is a vital way for us to let the energy of our emotions move through us so we can heal and learn from them. Researchers have found a myriad of benefits from crying, including relieving stress and pain, improving mood, and releasing toxins.[8]

Soon after my conversation about tears with Justin, I drove past my late mom's apartment on the way home from my gym. I sat at a red light reflecting on how much I missed her. I finally let myself cry. As tears blurred my vision, I pulled into a nearby gas station where I could safely park. I cried in my car, nonstop, for about half an hour. God's Spirit was present with me there, as he always is, but this time I felt the awe of his presence there.

When you ponder the word "emotion," think of energy in motion. God has designed our emotions to flow through us so we can learn and grow from the process. So instead of numbing ourselves to our feelings—which blocks the process of flow that God intends for those emotions—we must *feel* them. Rather than denying or repressing our God-given emotions, we need to connect with them to see what wonder they can show us.

Our emotions significantly impact our brainwaves.[9] When we hold inside our stressful emotions like fear and anger, our telomeres—the protective caps on our chromosomes—can shorten, leaving us vulnerable to disease and causing us to age faster.[10] The good news is when we practice prayer and meditation to manage stressful emotions well, our telomeres can lengthen, increasing our cellular protection.[11]

As we stop numbing ourselves and allow ourselves to feel and express our emotions honestly, we can sense the wonder God hides in plain sight all around us. Our emotions (and the thoughts that lead to them) are powerful, so, if we focus them with positive intentions as happens during prayer, we may experience great awe. Experiments show when small groups express positive emotions together with a common intention (such as healing), awe-inspiring events can happen as a result.[12]

Usually, the types of emotions we try to numb ourselves against are painful feelings. Pain signals something needs attention from us. When we try to avoid feeling pain through numbing methods, we miss valuable lessons like discovering God's strength in our weakness and developing compassion for others. Ironically, pain we numb ourselves against can often lead us to awe, if we're courageous enough to open those doors.

Our tears show us God cares about our sorrow and will use our pain to accomplish good purposes when we trust him to do so. One of the shortest verses in the Bible is "Jesus wept" (John 11:35) and refers to Jesus's reaction to seeing his friend Lazarus's grave. God experienced no shortage of sorrow himself when he walked on Earth in the flesh, and he is deeply concerned about the pain his beloved children go through. He has something valuable to teach us as we struggle with sorrow—something we couldn't learn without going through it, which will empower us to experience the wonder of God's love.

## Plan Wonder Walks and Other Wonder Breaks

Wonder breaks are periods of time to include in our schedules regularly, for the sole purpose of tuning into the wonder around us. We're much more likely to notice wonder when we're intentionally looking for it—and to do so, we need to allocate time to take regular breaks from the distractions of everything else competing for our attention. We can turn just about any activity we enjoy into a wonder break.

My favorite way to take wonder breaks is by taking wonder walks. Whenever possible (and no matter what the weather conditions are), I include walks in my schedule to begin or end my day with wonder. This one simple habit has led to more awe-inspiring experiences than I can count.

One evening during a routine walk in my neighborhood, I saw something bright streaking through the sky, leaving an awesome trail of light behind it. I stared at the sky, transfixed, until the glow faded from sight. After returning home and searching the news online, I discovered I'd witnessed the flight of an Antares rocket attached to a Cygnus spacecraft, which had launched that afternoon from NASA's Wallops Flight Facility. The launch was visible in my part of Virginia as the spacecraft flew toward the International Space Station, where it would deliver supplies to astronauts. Other surprises I've encountered just recently during routine neighborhood walks include vibrantly colored sunrises and sunsets, a team of firefighters rescuing a cat from a tree, a group of people restoring a beautiful antique car, and flocks of geese flying in intricately choreographed formations.

When traveling anywhere, I've found many more wonderful experiences. One of my favorite places to walk around in is New York City, where the energy of so many people together in one place is palpable. I never know when I'm going to find a treasure there—from a huge comic book shop with amazing art inside to a restaurant serving the best soup I've ever tasted (the smell wafting out the windows drew me inside). Wonders wait for discovery in quiet, rural places as well. The simple yet profound wonders of nature are constantly available in any park.

Walking can increase awareness of wonder by relieving stress, improving mood, boosting creative inspiration, improving memory, and strengthening concentration, according to research.[13]

Anything is possible when walking around looking for wonder. Walking is free, and you can take a walk anytime and anywhere. You can incorporate walking into your schedule in flexible ways—from long nature hikes on weekends to brief walks near your office during your lunch break.

Walking is only one of countless options you can choose for wonder breaks. Research shows that by planning regular breaks into our schedules, we can optimize our ability to focus. When we're paying attention well, we can notice the wonder around us. A study[14] found taking brief mental breaks from working on prolonged tasks significantly improved people's performance on those tasks. The breaks empowered them to focus well by giving them the variety that their minds craved.

Another study[15] showed people's minds are still highly active when they take breaks from work. During those breaks, neural scanners showed different regions of their brains lit up than those that lit up while they were working. Breaks where they were free to let their minds wander helped them notice and process thoughts and feelings they didn't focus on during work.

Every day is a new opportunity to manage our stress with help from God, who can empower us to feel and learn from our emotions in ways that lead to awe. My pastor often talks about living "in the yes position to God."

The choice to open ourselves to whatever messages God wants to communicate to us—and to respond to them with faithful action—encourages God to reach out to us more. Whenever we notice that happening, we experience wonder. Numbing ourselves emotionally is like freezing ourselves in a block of ice. We lose our ability to feel or move, which causes us to miss awe. God's passionate love is like a fire that can melt even the thickest ice away from our souls. Whenever we're ready to open our hearts, God will meet us with the fire of his love. Hebrews 12:28–29 urges us to approach God "with reverence and awe, for our God is a consuming fire." Opening our hearts to God is the first step to breaking free of numbness so we can experience more wonder.

## QUESTIONS TO PONDER FOR WONDER

1. How are you currently numbing yourself emotionally, and how can you start breaking those habits?
2. What painful feelings do you have blocked within you? What can you do to start putting those emotions into motion—crying or something else that will help you express them?
3. When stress triggers you to numb your feelings, how can you resist that temptation and instead go directly to God for peace?
4. What are you currently devoting your emotions to most strongly? What changes do you need to make to look for fulfillment in the only reliable source, God?
5. How can you plan wonder breaks (like wonder walks) into your schedule regularly? What types of wonder breaks would you like to pursue?

# Chapter 3

## Overcome Fear

My mood was as bleak as the cold, cloudy January weather when I heard the news: the transplant center had disqualified the wonderful man from our church who had planned to donate a kidney to Russ. Just before the scheduled surgery, the last test revealed a rare condition that forced our friend and donor to pull out. *Not again.* We had gone through many months of agonizing uncertainty about whether a kidney donor with a compatible blood type would help Russ. Several guys from our church had stepped forward, but they were either medically disqualified or dropped out for personal reasons. I tried not to let my hope go away with them. Yet here we were, with no way of moving forward with the lifesaving transplant Russ needed.

While driving to church for Honor's dance practice, my ruminating mind churned up all sorts of fears like toxic sediment set loose from the bottom of a polluted river. I pictured Russ dead and wondered how I would manage as a widow raising two children alone. Why did God let this happen? Does God really care? Can God really do anything to help?

I dropped Honor off at her practice, blinking back tears as a modern remix of an old hymn played in the background, praising God: "All I have needed thy hand hath provided—Great is thy faithfulness, God, unto me."[1]

Those lyrics felt like they were mocking me as I struggled to find God's faithfulness in this crisis. I sank down onto a bench on our church's playground and watched Justin play. He seemed so carefree sliding down a curvy slide— too young to realize life's curves can lead to an unexpected crash.

"Hi, I'm Jen. You look upset. How are you doing?" another mom asked as she sat down beside me. I hesitated, afraid that sharing my heavy burden would be too much for someone I'd just met.

As I was about to say, "I'm fine, thanks," and turn away, I decided to risk confiding in her. I poured out my heart to Jen and asked her if she'd pray for us to be able to find someone else willing to be a kidney donor. She and I prayed together. Then something even more wonderful happened. Jen asked her husband, Jody, to consider helping us. He got tested, was a match, and gave Russ a lifesaving kidney.

Driving toward the hospital on the morning of the transplant surgery, Russ and I watched a gorgeous sunrise emerge when the blackness of night dissipated and a blue sky appeared, streaked with purple, pink, and orange. Birds sitting on the branches of the white flowering dogwood trees we passed filled the warm spring air with songs that wafted through our car's rolled-down windows. All these signs of renewal filled us with a sense of excitement as we drove closer to the hospital. Relief and gratitude flooded over us as we pulled into the hospital's parking garage.

The road we had traveled before this morning had been a challenging and painful path. Then God led us to Jody, who heroically gave a part of his physical body to Russ. Jody's lifesaving good deed exemplified the truth described in 1 Corinthians 12:27: "Now you are the body of Christ, and each one of you is a part of it."

The great love Jody and Jen showed to us could only have been God's love working through them. There's no other way to explain why two people would want to do something so significant to help someone they hadn't even known before.

What if I had let fear prevent me from asking for the help our family needed? We all would have missed the awesome wonder of how God provided.

Our minds are battlegrounds between good and evil in this fallen world's ongoing spiritual war. Whenever we're attacked by fear, we can be sure that it does *not* come from God. Second Timothy 1:7 assures us, "For God has not given us a spirit of fear, but of power and of love and a sound mind." Fear stands in direct contrast to the faith that God calls us to embrace—the faith that leads to awe. When we allow ourselves to fall into fear, we miss wonder.

## Don't Miss Wonder Because of Worry

Looking at the massive stone walls of Notre Dame Cathedral as our tour boat passed, I reluctantly forced myself to turn away until our boat cruised away. I had wanted to visit the wondrous Paris cathedral for years, yet my family wasn't interested. I skipped it, reluctant to pressure them or split up to visit by myself. A "responsible" wife and mother wouldn't insist on going somewhere when her family didn't want to, would she? Worries about feeling like a "selfish" wife and mother prevented me from discussing Notre Dame again with my family during our trip, even as a heavy feeling of regret sank into my soul.

While flying home, I reassured myself there would be another chance to experience the wonder of Notre Dame, which had stood strong since medieval times. *It'll be there whenever I can come back to Paris.* Years later, another opportunity to visit Paris arose. This time, I made visiting Notre Dame a high priority: booking tour tickets and planning to attend a worship service there as well. Before we arrived in Paris, however, Notre Dame was devastated by fire and closed indefinitely. The fire made headlines around the world, as people grieved the damage to a place of awe, which had seemed indestructible. I'd finally overcome the worry that had caused me to miss out on Notre Dame's wonder years before, only to find it was too late to make up for lost time.

Worry can be a daunting challenge to overcome, since it's one of the most common ways we're tempted spiritually. The battle against worry has been the hardest spiritual battle for me to fight. I learned the bad habit of worrying as a child, after my parents' divorce and stepfamily stress made me feel insecure. I worried so much I sometimes fainted from panic attacks. As an adult, I continued to worry simply because I'd never learned how to let go of my bad habit. Worry seemed like a familiar friend, but it was an enemy, which robbed me of countless moments of awe over the years. I denied myself many experiences that called out to my soul—like visiting Notre Dame—whenever I worried about whether I could pursue them. Even though I loved God, my eyes were usually on my circumstances rather than on the God who is greater than any circumstances.

Worry keeps our souls asleep to the wonder around us precisely because our minds focus on circumstances rather than on God. Life in this fallen world includes an endless list of troubling possibilities—from major worries ("What if I lose my job?" "What if my health deteriorates?" "What if my spouse betrays me?" etc.) to minor worries ("What if I'm late for my appointment?" "What if this item I'm trying to order is out of stock?" "What if my friend doesn't want to join me at this event?"). We can let worry run rampant through our minds, but Jesus offers us a better way. In John 16:33, he tells us, "In me you may have peace. In this world you will have trouble. But take heart. I have overcome the world."

By connecting with Jesus for peace, we can discover the wonder of his constant presence with us. Joshua 1:9 encourages us, "Be strong and courageous. Do not be afraid; do not be discouraged, for the Lord your God will be with you wherever you go." We need to fight courageously against the fear and discouragement of worry. Reminding ourselves God is always with us can keep us grounded in reality, where we can grow beyond our fear and we grow closer to God. We don't have to pay attention when worry assaults our minds. We can choose to move our focus beyond our circumstances to God. We can look for the wonder of what God is doing in our lives.

Pursuing awe on purpose can push worry away. Research shows a sense of wonder can relieve the worry of waiting for uncertain news. Participants in a research study[2] had to wait to hear about something that was beyond their control—test results. The group who experienced awe from watching a video of a sunrise with instrumental music showed significantly less anxiety than others did. Experiencing wonder can relieve our worry. We simply must be willing to intentionally pursue wonder despite our fears. The journey of waking up to wonder can start in whatever circumstances and state of mind we're in, since God is always willing to meet us where we are.

Overcoming worry helps us discover the wonder that comes from experiencing God's peace. That peace only comes to us when we decide to stop worrying and start to trust God. St. Paul's words in Philippians 4:6–7 encourage us: "Do not be anxious about anything, but in every situation, by prayer and petition, with thanksgiving, present your requests to God. And the peace of God, which transcends all understanding, will guard your hearts and your minds in Christ Jesus." Worry doesn't have the power to prevent anything bad from happening in our lives, and worry has no power to accomplish anything positive. Therefore, worry is completely useless.

We can't stop anxiety from entering our minds, but we can ask God for help by turning our worries into prayers. Whenever we become aware we're worrying about something, we can pray immediately. The more we push worry out of our lives, the more our minds will be free to notice the wonder happening around us.

## DON'T MISS WONDER BECAUSE OF INSECURITY

My heartbeat raced as I listened to Cheryl tell our Bible study group a story about a wondrous experience. After her sister passed away in a car accident, Cheryl prayed for encouragement, and shortly afterward felt a hand on her shoulder and smelled her sister's favorite perfume. I also had a story to share of hope breaking through grief because of an encounter with wonder. However, I hesitated to share because of insecurity. Excuses for not speaking up ran through my mind. My story might seem weird to those listening. I might become too emotional while telling it. People might ask me questions about it that I couldn't answer. However, since Cheryl had boldly told her story, I decided to push insecurity aside and raised my hand to share next.

"On the day my mom passed away, I learned the news early in the morning, while I was still wearing a pajama top Mom had given me. Its bold blue colors and whimsical star and cloud shapes reminded me of Mom's adventurous personality. I only had half of the pajama set, though. The pants had been missing for many years. Mom had helped me look for them to no avail. We joked that someday they might show up if I ever cleaned out my messy closets. Soon after I heard of her death, I drove over to her apartment to reminisce. She kept a cedar chest by the foot of her bed to preserve family photos inside. When I opened the lid, I was shocked the first item I saw was my long-lost pajama bottoms!"

I anxiously scanned my fellow group members' faces for any signs of disapproval. They all seemed positive, so I continued. "Mom only kept photos in that chest over the years. Those pajama pants were out of place. When I lifted them out, I discovered they'd been placed on a greeting card. The card was blank inside, but the cover said: 'Thinking of you—until we meet again.'"

Bracing myself for awkward silence, I felt a rush of confidence when group members exclaimed that may have been a miraculous sign God sent to comfort me. Not only did they not find the story weird, but they told me they thought what had happened was wonderful.

Some group members told Cheryl and me that the risks we took in sharing our stories made them feel comfortable enough to tell their own stories of how God used wonder to encourage them in the midst of grief. Listening to each person's story filled me with awe. Driving home, I thanked God for the thought-provoking discussion we all had because we overcame insecurity to share stories with each other.

Why do we let insecurity prevent us from pursuing awe? That tends to happen when we're self-conscious rather than

God-conscious. Sometimes, self-consciousness is normal. Here's the challenge, though—If we're preoccupied with ourselves, we can miss God at work right there with us. If we're focused too much on what other people may be thinking about us, we'll miss what God wants to do through our lives—including powerful experiences of awe.

The negative self-talk going through our minds when we feel insecure doesn't reflect what God thinks about us. From God's perspective, each of us is a person of infinite value who is worthy of love. While living in a society that can make us feel we are not enough—attractive enough, smart enough, rich enough, or failing to measure up in some other way—we must be intentional about viewing ourselves the way God sees us.

The Bible declares all believers can "approach God's throne of grace with confidence" (Hebrews 4:16). The security God offers us through relationships with Jesus can never be shaken.

As we walk away from insecurity and toward confidence, we'll wake up to the wonder around us simply because we've given ourselves permission to look for it. The more we realize we deserve to experience a life of wonder, the more we can pursue and enjoy the wonder God freely gives.

## WIPE AWAY FEAR TO SEE WONDER MORE CLEARLY

A sunset lit up the sky outside our living room window with rosy streaks of color. Bathed in the sunset's light, two squirrels chased each other around the trunk of a tree. The wonder called me to take a break from my to-do list and soak in the beauty before me, but the grime obscured my view. White blotches blurred the shapes and muted the colors outside. Squinting didn't help me see any better. I could see how the dirt we had allowed to accumulate was blocking me from seeing something wonderful.

Stepping outside, the view became clear. Now I could see the squirrels' tiny claws against the tree's rough bark as they ran around its trunk. The sky's colors came vividly alive, casting our whole yard into a rosy glow. What had looked like just an intriguing blob of color from behind the dirty window now appeared as distinct colors—lavender, pink, and orange—all reflected in the puffy clouds whose shapes stood out in wondrous detail.

Fear covers our souls with grime, preventing us from noticing the awe around us.

If fear has accumulated in your soul, here's a process for wiping it away: Pay attention to persistent fears in your life. Do you struggle with worrisome thoughts? Are you allowing insecurity to limit your experiences in life? Are you infected with anger because of people or situations you fear? Are you struggling with a bad habit or even an addiction that fuels your fear? Pray about every fear specifically. Ask God to help you trust him more with each of those concerns. Whenever negative thoughts enter your mind, purposefully replace them with positive ones. Whenever you're tempted to slide back into a fearful behavior, ask God to empower you to resist and overcome temptation. Seek to know and love God more. The closer you become to God, the less you'll struggle with fear.

Don't spend another day letting fear rob you of the wonder God wants you to enjoy. In John 14:16, Jesus calls the Holy Spirit our "advocate" (the person of the Trinity who will guide us to make wise choices and help us in even the toughest situations). You can kick fear-based attitudes out of your mind with the Holy Spirit's help. Whenever someone or something triggers fear in you, choose to pray about that fear instead of wallowing in it. Intentionally release the fear you feel to God and invite him to help you in the circumstances behind that fear. God will always meet you where you are when you reach out to him, and you'll discover awe in the process.

## QUESTIONS TO PONDER FOR WONDER

1. What specific types of fears run through your mind on a regular basis? How can you start praying regularly about what scares you the most often?

2. How have you let worry rob you of some wonderful experiences you now regret missing? The next time you're anxious about something you want to enjoy, how can you move forward—despite feeling afraid—to pursue wonder?

3. How have you let insecurity limit how much you allow yourself to pursue wonder? How can you build your confidence from God's love for you, and start pursuing the wonder God wants you to enjoy?

4. How have you let fear prevent you from noticing and appreciating the wonder around you? How can you work with the Holy Spirit to overcome fear?

5. The next time you experience spiritual warfare in your mind, what can you do to turn away from fear and turn toward faith?

# Chapter 4
## Pursue Lifelong Learning

A group of five middle-school students asked my father, a senior citizen, what his life was like as a student years ago. Dad replied with some interesting stories and added, "Even now, though, I still consider myself to be a student. I'm a lifelong learner." Dad was participating in the annual Eyewitness to History Day at my son's school. More than one hundred people shared their historical stories with the students in interviews that day—a man who had survived a World War II concentration camp and become a rabbi afterward, a woman who had been a first responder during the 9/11 terrorist attack rescues, and others who each had their own uniquely powerful experiences. The interviewees shared some profound lessons with the students, but the learning that day flowed in both directions. Often, interviewees told the students how grateful they were to learn about their young lives, as well.

Most Americans (73 percent) consider themselves to be lifelong learners, a Pew Research Center survey[1] revealed, because they participated in some sort of learning activity during the past year such as reading a book, participating in a group related to their interests or hobbies, attending a conference, taking an online course, etc. Their top reason for seeking new learning experiences was "to learn something that would help them make their life more interesting and full"—something that wonder empowers people to do. One of the top benefits of lifelong learning, survey respondents said, was it "opened up new perspectives about their lives," which is also something that happens when people experience wonder. Wonder can lead to learning, and learning can lead to more wonder, research has found.[2]

Pursuing lifelong learning is a powerful way to discover wonder, which we can block by not pursuing some of the learning opportunities God brings to us. Sometimes our minds are open, which helps us notice and appreciate awe. Yet at other times, our minds are closed to learning something new.

## Let Go of Attitudes that Block Learning

We miss wonder if we miss the lifelong learning God has in store for us. Opening our minds and hearts to learning something new always connects us with wonder, since awe and learning are connected. Often, when we pay attention to our need for wonder—like children do—we gain the motivation we need to pursue learning to fulfill our need. A research study found wonder is what drives meaningful learning because it is connected to beauty, sensitivity, and secure attachment.[3]

Wonder is essential for creativity, which is at the heart of learning. A sense of wonder has compelled creative people throughout history to create artistic masterpieces and scientific inventions. Awe fuels creativity by empowering people to engage in the present with what may be possible in the future, a research study found.[4] Another research study showed awe inspires creativity by shaking people's confidence in their existing knowledge, motivating them to learn more as a result.[5]

What attitudes are currently blocking you from taking advantage of the learning opportunities God brings into your life? Are you stuck in routines that limit how many new experiences you include in your schedule? Are you avoiding risks you need to take to learn, because you're afraid of what might happen if you took those risks? Are you so tired you're not putting much energy into learning what interests you? Whatever obstacles you face, you can rely on God to help you overcome them and become a lifelong learner. Jesus promises in John 14:26 that the Holy Spirit will be a "Counselor" who "will teach you all things." The first step in discovering wonder through learning is asking for the Holy Spirit's help.

The next step is to pay attention to your God-given curiosity. A team led by George Mason University researchers developed a five-dimensional model of curiosity. The second dimension ("Joyous Exploration") describes how people can express their curiosity by pursuing wonder through lifelong learning. People who are curious in a joyous exploration way agreed with these statements: "I view challenging situations as an opportunity to grow and learn." "I seek out situations where it is likely that I will have to think in depth about something." "I enjoy learning about subjects that are unfamiliar to me," and "I find it fascinating to learn new information."[6]

If you aren't fully engaging your curiosity right now, God can help you open your mind more. All you have to do is ask. Then shake up your routine and reset your thinking. Try eating some different foods, talking with a few people you don't know well, changing the media you watch and listen to, driving a different route through your community, and anything else in your routine where you've fallen into a rut and can refresh your perspective through some simple changes.

Finally, open both your mind and your heart to pursuing wonder, which runs deeper than just curiosity. We can be curious but not be motivated enough to act on that curiosity. Wonder, however, gives us powerful motivation to pursue the learning opportunities God brings us.

## READ MORE

Lifting some new books out of a box, I savored the tangy scent of new ink and paper and the sight of glistening covers filled with colorful illustrations. I set a pile of books on a table and tried to walk away. We had lots of boxes to unpack, and my fellow volunteers and I didn't have much time to set up the school book fair. Browsing the books wouldn't be an efficient use of time, but I couldn't help myself. Lingering over the books, I chose a copy of the Guinness World Records and began flipping through the pages. Amazing facts seemed to pop off each page, giving me a sense of wonder: the largest bubblegum bubble blown (20 inches), the fastest car's land speed (763 miles per hour), the most decimal places of Pi memorized (70,000), the longest duration balancing on four fingers (19.23 seconds), the longest distance swum underwater with one breath (656 feet), the largest gathering of people wearing false moustaches (6,471), the loudest purr by a domestic cat (67.8 decibels), the most tricks performed by a dog in one minute (49), the longest butterfly migration (2,880 miles), and many more.

Years had passed since I attended school. Yet I was still enjoying learning from these books intended for students. Reading can be wonderful at any age.

Research shows reading can powerfully improve our well-being. A study[7] found just thirty minutes of reading for pleasure a day leads to many benefits, including *more* confidence, creativity, empathy for others, community spirit, cultural awareness, good quality sleep, and *less* stress, loneliness, isolation, and anxiety.

I look forward to reading nearly every evening. Reading helps me relax and reflect so I can learn well. While I read a diverse variety of books, I'm especially drawn to those exploring the connections between science and spirituality, such as near-death experience (NDE) reports. NDE stories and research spark awe in my soul. Thanks to the wonder of reading, I don't have to die and return to learn inspiring information about the afterlife.

We can always discover wonder within the words of books. "The more that you read, the more things you will know. The more that you learn, the more places you'll go," Dr. Seuss wrote in his famous children's book, *I Can Read with My Eyes Shut!*[8] That's true for us adults as much as it is for children. No matter what types of books we read—in any genre of nonfiction or fiction—we can expand our minds with learning that leads us to awe.

## ENGAGE IN CONVERSATIONS MORE

Swallowing a bite of salad, I broke into a fit of laughter in my company's employee cafeteria. "I don't actually *want* to see them naked," I told my colleagues gathered around a circular table with me. "But it should be an interesting experience."

"Hey, Henry, join us," one coworker called out to another who was strolling by with his tray. "Whitney is planning to visit a nudist colony in a few weeks."

Henry raised his eyebrows at me.

"My husband's great aunt and uncle live in a retirement nudist colony in Florida," I said.

"Naked, elderly, sunburned bodies—who wouldn't want to see that?"

Everyone at our table erupted into uproarious laughter at Henry's sarcastic tone. After the guffaws quieted down, another colleague spoke. "Are you planning to join them?" she asked me. "Are you and Russ planning to take off your clothes when you visit the colony?"

"Um …" my words trailed off into an uncomfortable silence.

"I don't think they could require that, could they?" someone else asked.

"Well, they don't require it, but Russ said it's considered polite to take your clothes off when you visit—as a way of showing respect for their culture."

"Really?" several people exclaimed at once. Then a rapid-fire discussion followed, as various colleagues weighed in on the topic of nudity.

"Nudity seems disrespectful to me."

"Why? That's natural. That's how God made us."

"Right," a colleague said. "Adam and Eve were naked but not ashamed. Isn't that what the Bible says?"

"But didn't they put fig leaves on after the fall?"

"Not because God told them to. They were trying to hide from God because they were ashamed—they'd lost their innocence."

For the next several weeks at every workday lunch, my colleagues and I debated the pros and cons of going *au naturel* with other people who have wholesome and respectful approaches to nudity. We shared our opinions openly, discussed theology together, and looked up Bible verses at the table. Together, we sought God's wisdom on the topic of nudity—and as we broke down conversational walls with each other, we took a God-focused approach to other topics too. We shared what God was doing in our lives and prayed for each other's day-to-day concerns. Our lunches became times to worship together, even though we were gathered in an ordinary workplace cafeteria.

What happened when I visited the nudist colony? I kept my clothes on—but only because our nudist hosts told me they like non-nudist guests to stay clothed to feel comfortable. My work colleagues were disappointed when I returned to tell them I hadn't gone nude as planned. But our God-focused discussions continued over weekday meals in our office building.

Engaging in conversations with others is a powerful way to learn and discover wonder in the process. Research suggests conversations can help people learn in several key ways: understanding more about a topic, answering a question, and solving a problem.[9]

What topics are you wondering about, and who can you talk with about those topics to learn something new? Every interaction with someone else—in person, over the phone, or even online—is an opportunity to learn something from that person. Listening to others' stories, discussing interesting information, and opening your mind to new perspectives can teach you something valuable. Ask God to show you how you can start pursuing more conversations that lead to wonder.

## TRAVEL MORE

Rain pelted my face, mixing with my tears as I said a prayer, held an urn out in front of me, and turned it upside down. Ashes streamed out into a lashing wind that nearly knocked me off the slippery step where I stood.

Watching these ashes—all that remained of my mom's earthly body—blow into the wind and fall into the Irish Sea, I heard a shrill call and looked up. A seagull flew over where I stood on Dollymount Strand beach north of Dublin. The bird met my gaze as it flapped its wings hard in the wind and continued its journey through the gray sky. It reminded me of my mom's determination to take a journey whenever she could. Mom loved to travel, and she instilled that love in my sister and me. A single mother, Mom couldn't afford to take us on many international trips, but she often took us on domestic trips, and discussed world cultures with us over dinner at ethnic restaurants. Shortly before she passed away, Mom had challenged me to travel as much as possible—starting with this journey to Ireland to scatter her ashes in the waters of her beloved ancestral home.

Now, I said another prayer for her and walked off the promontory to a taxi waiting on the beach. On the ride back to Dublin, the taxi whizzed by pubs, bookstores, shops, and a massive soccer stadium. The more I saw, the more excitement welled up within me. I had two whole weeks in front of me to explore Ireland. God willing, I'd have opportunities to travel to other nations, as well. Mom's past words to me echoed in my mind. "You learn so much when you travel that you always return home changed for the better."

Thankfully, in the years since then, I've been able to travel with my family to many countries around the world. We prioritize travel in our budget and schedule as much as possible. Why? Because every trip enriches our souls deeply with learning and wonder we couldn't experience at home.

Traveling can lead to wonder, but stress can cause people to forget that, according to a research study on travel and wonder.[10] Trips which are relaxing often lead to wonder, the study showed, because traveling gives people opportunities to step away from their daily demands, surprises them, challenges them, and empowers them to learn through new experiences.[11] Travel empowers people to learn in several different ways. Research shows trip experiences can positively affect travelers' perception, awareness, imagination, and reasoning—all of which help them learn.[12]

Wonder is waiting for you everywhere on our planet. You can discover it by learning something new on trips. Traveling doesn't have to be expensive or time-consuming. Even simple trips to nearby places can teach us something and spark our wonder. Saint Augustine said, "The world is a book and those who do not travel read only one page."[13] If you're not traveling on a regular basis, you're missing out on lifelong learning that leads to wonder.

## PAY ATTENTION TO DREAMS

One evening, after I'd prayed about how much I missed my late mother and asked God to send my love to her, I dreamed about Mom. I was in awe of this gift from God. Sometimes God will allow us to experience a vision from someone in heaven, for a specific purpose. We should never reach out to contact our departed loved ones ourselves, since attempting to communicate with them outside of God's care could be dangerous. But we can pray for God to send them a message, and we can trust that if God wants us to hear a message from them, he will allow a communication at the right time and in the right way.

In my dream, Mom looked like a young adult again, glowing with good health instead of ravaged by cancer as she had looked when she passed away. We met in a setting that looked like a busy airport. Mom said she was enjoying learning a lot in heaven. Laughing, she told me heaven isn't anything like the boring cartoon depictions of people sitting around passively on clouds. Instead, she said, there is always something wonderful to do and something new to learn.

After a few minutes of conversation, Mom told me she had to go, but she would be watching the rest of my life and supporting me in prayer. Then she ascended an escalator, looking back at me and saying the escalator represented her learning process. As we expressed love for each other while she rode upward, I felt the love roll over me like an overwhelmingly powerful wave. She reached the top of the escalator and stepped off to somewhere I couldn't see.

Through dreams, we can access wonder through learning even when we're asleep.

When we dream, we can connect with inspiration beyond the time and space boundaries we live in while awake. The distractions, which may have blocked us from noticing wonder during the day, clear out of our minds. We can then access subconscious thoughts and feelings. All dreams help our minds process information. Dreaming can help people learn by improving their memory and showing them how to solve problems, according to a Harvard Medical School research study of college students.[14]

Some dreams go beyond processing information by giving us access to the wonder of direct spiritual messages. The Bible often describes God sending messages to people through dreams. A few examples are the prophet Jacob dreaming of angels going back and forth between heaven and earth, Joseph's dreams as well as the Magi's dreams from the Christmas story, and Pontius Pilate's wife's dream from the Easter story.

You never know when God may reach out to you through a dream. If you believe in the possibility, and if you're seeking God, you're in the best position to notice divine dream messages when they do come. The ways God may communicate with you in dreams include:

- **Sending you creative inspiration:** God may send you an innovative idea through a dream. Many scientific breakthroughs and artistic projects throughout history have resulted from dreams. For example, physicist Niels Bohr, who won a Nobel Prize for discovering the structure of the atom, dreamed about the structure first and then confirmed his hypothesis through lab tests.

- **Guiding you to solve problems:** Solutions for problems in your life may come to you in your dreams as God answers your prayers for guidance. Inventor Madame C. J. Walker prayed for help solving the problem of her hair falling out after a scalp infection. She dreamed of an angelic man who showed her the specific ingredients she needed to create a hair care product that would help. After she woke from the dream, Madame Walker got to work on the product, which successfully solved hair problems not just for her, but for many other people. She became a millionaire in the process.

- **Healing you from past pain:** You may receive divine healing for your soul while you're dreaming about something that caused you pain. Famous adventurer Bear Grylls said he dreamed about falling for eighteen months straight after he broke his back in a skydiving accident, and those dreams helped him recover emotionally and regain his courage.

- **Warning you about an issue that needs attention:** Through dreams, God may warn you about something important but dangerous to ignore, such as an unhealthy habit (like an addiction) or a person who needs your help. Bestselling novelist Stephen King has said his nightmares not only give him ideas for his horror books, they also act like mirrors showing him issues he should address in his life. Sometimes divine warning dreams predict a future event, as well. For instance, former US president Abraham Lincoln had a vivid dream he was going to be assassinated shortly before it happened.
- **Encouraging you with peace or confidence:** Perhaps the most common type of divine message delivered during dreams is encouragement. Encouraging dreams give you peace when you're worried about something or confidence when you're facing a risk God wants you to take. Olympian Edwin Moses reported he had a series of encouraging dreams prior to a 400-meter hurdling race that gave him both the peace and confidence he needed to run well. The dreams featured numbers indicating the race's date and his running time. Moses broke a world record when he ran the race.

We can learn profound lessons from the wonder of our dreams when we pay close attention to them.

Dreams are full of symbols to allow our subconscious mind to work through the process of analyzing the information our conscious mind neglects to deal with while we're awake. Whenever we notice patterns occurring in our dreams in which the same symbol shows up multiple times, we need to pray about those patterns after waking up to figure out what they mean.

We can pursue awe through our dreams. By setting an intention to dream about a topic, we plant a seed for that thought to grow into a dream. By praying about a specific subject at bedtime, we invite God to send a dream message in response to that prayer. By recording what we remember about our dreams soon after waking (when we're in what psychologists call the "hypnagogic state" of transition, with our conscious and subconscious minds working together), we create valuable records to study and learn from dream patterns. By thinking and praying about the images in our dreams, we can learn from their symbolic meaning for us. By applying what we learn from dream insights to our waking lives, we can experience the wonder of closer relationships with God.

## Look Forward to Discovering Wonder through Learning

Every new day God gives us to live is full of valuable opportunities to learn. When we remind ourselves of that, our excitement to be lifelong learners can grow. Looking to the examples of others who prioritize lifelong learning can also inspire us. One of the world's most famous inventors, engineer and physicist Nikola Tesla, was a lifelong learner whose faith and wonder fueled his pursuit of lifelong learning.

One day when Tesla was a teenager, he and some friends went hiking through mountains during winter. They played with snowballs, competing to see who could build the best snowball. They had an experience that instilled awe in Tesla at the wonder of nature's energy.

"Suddenly a ball was seen to go beyond the limit, swelling to enormous proportions until it became as big as a house and plunged thundering into the valley below with a force that made the ground tremble," Tesla recalled in his autobiography. "For weeks afterwards, the picture of the avalanche was before my eyes, and I wondered how anything so small could grow to such an immense size. … when, years later, I took up the experimental study of mechanical and electrical resonance, I was keenly interested from the start. Possibly, had it not been for that early powerful impression, I might not have followed up that little spark I obtained with my coil and never developed my best invention."[15]

That invention was the alternating current motor, which revolutionized how humanity generated and transmitted electrical power.

As Tesla kept paying attention to his sense of awe, he kept seeking the source of that wonder—God—and learning more in the process. "The gift of mental power comes from God, Divine Being, and if we concentrate our minds on that truth, we become in tune with this great power," he said. Tesla believed faith and science complement each other and help people learn. He pointed out: "We cannot help wondering how profoundly wise and scientific and how immensely practical the Christian religion is … Thus, we are inspired both by Christianity and science to do our utmost toward increasing the performance of mankind."[16]

Tesla never stopped looking forward to new learning opportunities, and he encouraged others to keep learning and moving humanity forward with their own contributions. "The wonders of yesterday are today common occurrences," he wrote.[17]

Stop missing out on the learning opportunities in your own life and start a habit of pursuing lifelong learning that can lead you to awe. Jesus, who was often called "Rabboni" (which means a master teacher) by people during his earthly life, invites us to learn from him: "Take my yoke upon you and *learn from me*, for I am gentle and humble in heart, and you will find rest for your souls" (Matthew 11:29, emphasis added). Everything you learn from God will open your mind to the wonder of his work in our world.

## QUESTIONS TO PONDER FOR WONDER

1. When was the last time you learned something that ignited a spark of wonder within you? What is something else you've been wondering, and why would you like to learn more about it?

2. What are your favorite genres of books to read and why? What types of articles do you most enjoy? Do you read in print or online, or listen to audio recordings? How could you make more time for reading in your schedule on a regular basis?

3. Who are five different people you know and would like to learn more about their life stories? When can you schedule a time to call or meet them for a good conversation?

4. Where are some places you'd like to visit in your local area? What are some faraway trips you'd like to take? How can you change your lifestyle to start traveling on a regular basis?

5. What is one recurring dream about which you would like to learn more? How can you study that dream's potential meaning and apply its wisdom to your life?

# Chapter 5

## Use Your Senses

As I looked across the bioluminescent lagoon Laguna Grande in Puerto Rico, pinpricks of light on the water's surface seemed to mirror the stars above. A chorus of coqui frogs sang to each other from the dark trees surrounding the lagoon. I swirled a twig in the water to trigger the lagoon's one-celled organisms called dinoflagellates to display their light. Glowing ripples of light shone in the water from wherever I moved the twig. The coquis' playful calls floated through the air, adding to my joy. Curious, I traced the letters of my name in the water and found I could really write with light. Each letter appeared for a few seconds before fading. Awestruck at the wonder around me, I wrote "Thank you, God" in the water.

We can use all our physical senses—seeing, hearing, smelling, tasting, and touching—as tools for accessing awe that enriches us spiritually. The more we integrate the spiritual and physical aspects of our sensory experiences, the more we can notice and appreciate wonder.

### THE WONDER OF SIGHT

The picture of a girl riding a bicycle was rudimentary—simply a stick figure on a basic bike frame, drawn with broad crayon strokes. Her simple drawing was nowhere near as artistically inspiring as the art I'd seen in museums. Yet the picture opened a door to wonder for me when I looked at her work while volunteering in a kindergarten class at my children's elementary school. That drawing represented the joy of adventure, which the artist (a student) wanted to celebrate. Many of the children were still learning to write, so drawing was the primary way they expressed their thoughts and feelings on their school journal pages. Their drawings were portals to wonder for them, inspiring them to express what was in their minds. Patterns emerged, such as this one from a girl who often drew herself riding her bicycle to share her excitement for exploring the world.

The kids experienced wonder by engaging their visual senses through drawing. I experienced wonder from seeing what emerged on paper when they worked. Often, they wanted to talk about their drawings with me. Those simple drawings always reflected subjects that mattered deeply to the students. They ran the emotional gamut, as well— from a child who celebrated his favorite food (pizza) often in his journal to a child whose parents were divorcing and frequently depicted his family together on a sinking ship.

Viewing art can promote joyful feelings of awe. Research[2] shows, immediately after people start looking at art, their brains release the chemical dopamine. Dopamine is associated with feelings of intense pleasure.

Examples of some awesome sights we can seek out include sunrises and sunsets, flowers, the beauty of loved ones' faces, fashionable clothing, handcrafted furniture, natural landscapes at parks, and more.

Try these ideas for developing your sense of sight to experience more awe:

1. Go to a busy public place (such as a mall) and watch people for a while. See how much interesting information you can learn just by watching them.
2. Visit a local park and capture your impressions of the natural scenes there. Take photos or draw what you see that inspires you.
3. Visit an art gallery with a friend and discuss each other's observations of the artwork.

## THE WONDER OF HEARING

Dancing to the pulsating beats of an electronic dance song in a Zumba class, I felt the music's rhythms so deeply my heartbeat and breathing synced up to the song. The music seemed to become a part of my body and resonated in my soul as well. My worries evaporated and joy rushed in. I felt connected to my classmates through the music— enveloped together into the sounds we heard. While we danced in sync with the song's beats, we focused on enjoying the present moment in a wonderful experience of creative flow. Research reveals music moves our brains to pay full attention to the present moment,[3] which in turn empowers us to notice the wonder around us.

Music is an especially powerful tool for engaging your senses to wake up to wonder. Since everyone and everything in the universe vibrates, the sound vibrations of music resonate too. Music is a universal language that transcends all barriers between people, allowing us to communicate deep feelings with each other.

At George Mason University, our Center for the Advancement of Well-Being helped create a minor in music and well-being[4] that is open to all students—even those with no musical experience—because everyone can tap into music's well-being power. Music can help people experience awe through transformative experiences together, said Dr. Linda Monson, director of Mason's School of Music. "We can have meaningful communication happen through wordless sound," she said. "Music really *is* community because we bring people together through sound. There's a shared experience that moves us together by creating transformative beauty and peace. We are practicing an art form that connects to each of us as full human beings."[5]

While music is especially wonderful, there are countless other ways to experience awe by engaging with the sounds around us. Laughter, birds chirping, rain falling against windows, bells ringing, a fire crackling, wind blowing through tree leaves, food sizzling in a pan, popcorn popping, people cheering at a sports game, thunder, a clock ticking, a carbonated drink fizzing, and more can lead us to wonder.

Try these ideas for developing your sense of hearing to experience more awe:

1. Sit outside and close your eyes. Listen to sounds and make note of the different kinds—from traffic noises to bird calls.
2. Enjoy a wide variety of music genres (rock, jazz, country, classical, etc.) rather than sticking just with your favorite type of music. As you listen, see if you can identify each of the different musical instruments in each song.
3. Before you go to sleep, when your mind is relaxed, notice which sounds you hadn't noticed before.

## THE WONDER OF SMELL

Hiking with my family in California's Sequoia National Park, I looked up to the crowns of the giant trees but didn't pay enough attention to my path on the ground. Soon, I'd bumped into a log and heard a grunt. What I saw after that was one of the biggest shocks of my life. I'd woken a napping grizzly bear. The massive bear was splayed out on the ground while resting one of its paws and its head on the log. Now the bear's deep brown eyes were looking directly into mine. I stood mesmerized, unable to speak. But Russ, Honor, and Justin yelled in alarm when they realized we were face to face with a wild creature, which could turn us all into snacks that summer afternoon.

The bear seemed just as surprised as we were. Slowly, he raised his head from the log and began sniffing us. The bulbous black nose moved around methodically as he gathered scent data on us. Two huge nostrils sucked in air. Huffing and puffing sounds emanated from the bear's snout. I sent a silent, one-word prayer to God in that moment. *Help!* I'd read turning away from a bear and running is wrong. That only invites a bear to chase. So I started walking backward while maintaining eye contact with the grizzly and whispering to my family to do the same. As we shuffled slowly away, the bear's enormous nose continued to sniff the air around us, but the bear didn't rise completely to his feet. He simply watched us carefully as we backed out of view. What did the bear think of our fragrance? Covered in sunscreen and bug spray, maybe we were too stinky to be appealing bear snacks. There may have been a different reason the grizzly bear refrained from attacking us. Whatever the reason, I was grateful God had answered my urgent prayer and allowed us to escape.

As we continued our hike through the forest, we were giddy with joy—from both the wonder of encountering a wild grizzly and the wonder of emerging from that encounter unharmed. Laughing about the bear's energetic nose, we impersonated it by sniffing the air ourselves. Delightful scents filled the forest—butterscotch aromas from the ponderosa pine trees, woody fragrances from the sequoia trees, and earthy odors from the fern undergrowth. Overall, the air was invigorating to breathe—a fresh blend of scents that made us feel good each time we inhaled.

Forest air contains aromatic plant compounds called phytoncides. Plants release these natural chemicals into the air to protect themselves from insects. Research shows when people breathe in phytoncides, they can experience many benefits, including stronger immune systems that reduce their risk of cancer,[6] greater physical energy and mental concentration, lower blood pressure, and less anxiety.[6] A practice called forest bathing, which involves walking inside forests to soak in their cleansing health benefits, is now becoming a popular practice. Beyond forests, any natural outdoor location offers a plethora of invigorating scents to enjoy—from salty air at a beach to flowers in a garden.

We can also wake up our sense of smell indoors. When Honor was a preschooler, she asked to go shopping with me for some new candles for our home. I told her she could choose a few candles with her favorite fragrances. She began methodically sniffing candles at the store, row by row, until she had sniffed *every one* of the more than three hundred candles in stock. After the first twenty or so, I was already losing patience and telling her to hurry up and choose some.

"Wait," she replied simply, continuing her olfactory adventure. Annoyed, I paced around the aisles while watching her. Her face lit up with awe every time she breathed in a new scent—crisp linen, apple pie, rain showers, eucalyptus, gingerbread, spruce, raspberry, lavender, pumpkin, sage, rose, jasmine, vanilla, and many more.

Soon, concerned I was missing out on a valuable experience, I joined her. Time seemed to stand still as I gave myself over to the wonder of savoring each scent. I don't know how long we were in that candle store, since we didn't bother keeping track, but we spent the time together well.

Our sense of smell can usher us into wonderful experiences in a myriad of ways. Scents we can focus on to discover awe include roses, freshly baked bread or chocolate chip cookies, a new car, an evergreen tree, coffee, spices like vanilla and cinnamon, fruit like lemons and oranges, scented candles, leather, and more.

Try these ideas for developing your sense of smell to experience more awe:

1. Enjoy a meal with family and friends. While you're eating, discuss the aromas of the food and why those aromas are appealing.
2. Spend some time in a candle store sniffing the many different varieties of candles there. Which ones do you like the most? Which ones do you dislike? What memories do the scents trigger in your mind?
3. Take a walk outside right after it rains (when the air is freshly clean). Pay attention to the various odors you smell and consider how those scents make you feel.

## THE WONDER OF TASTE

Vegetable broth bubbled in multiple pots as the girls in Honor's Girl Scout troop cooked a stew together. The stew featured an outlandish variety of vegetables—a fresh version of every item the girls wanted to contribute—potatoes, onions, carrots, zucchini, celery, plum tomatoes, cabbage, squash, mushrooms, red peppers, spinach, green beans, lentil beans, peas, and corn. We seasoned the stew with even more ingredients—chopped garlic cloves, parsley, salt, and pepper. There was such a riot of food in this stew the girls joked the concoction would probably taste like nothing, with all the different flavors covering each other.

Once we tasted the meal, however, the result was just the opposite. Each flavor complemented the others. Every bite of this wonderful stew brought many layers of delight to our taste buds. The girls, who were earning nutrition badges through this activity, tasted how delicious healthy eating can be.

"Wow," one girl exclaimed, "God is so creative."

"Yeah, I always wondered why he made weird-looking stuff like squash. But squash tastes good," another marveled. "I still don't like celery, though."

"That's okay," someone else responded. "You've got lots of other options."

"God is generous too," I pointed out while stirring the bounty of vegetables in my bowl.

God could have chosen to create us without the need to eat. Or he could have created just one kind of food that fulfilled all our nutritional needs—like he did temporarily with the manna he provided for ancient Israelites in the desert. Instead, God chose to create a huge variety and abundance of food for us to grow, prepare, and eat however we like. Thanks to that, we can (and should) *enjoy* our food. Our taste buds remind us that every eating experience can open a door to wonder in our lives.

A research study[7] found that children who received education about their physical senses were more likely than others to try unfamiliar foods. By increasing the variety in their diets, the children experienced the wonder of new tastes. The more we think about our taste buds, the more we can be inspired to try new recipes for foods and drinks. As we explore, we can discover all sorts of wonder from the creative culinary options God has made available to us.

God has created a myriad of ingredients we can enjoy in foods and beverages that delight our senses.

Try these ideas for developing your sense of taste to experience more awe:

1. Each time you buy groceries, buy a kind of food or drink you've never tasted. Whenever you discover something you like, buy more and share it with your family.
2. Eat out at different types of ethnic restaurants. Learn about various cultures around the world by eating their cuisine.
3. Cook some new recipes regularly to enjoy for breakfast, lunch, and dinner.

## THE WONDER OF TOUCH

As I read on a sofa, our long-haired cat, Whiskers, jumped into my lap and laid down to be petted. Her soft, wispy fur felt like cotton candy in my hands as I stroked her back. Her bushy tail swept across my lap from side to side like a gentle feather. She kneaded her paws, sending tiny pinpricks through my legs with her claws. Then, she began purring. As the vibrations of her purrs radiated through me, I felt the wonder of love pets so beautifully offer people. The simple act of petting my cat put me in touch with significant joy and a sense of transcendence. I felt centered in God's love while touching one of his creatures. While Whiskers purred, I sent a silent prayer of thanks to God.

A review of research[8] into the benefits of physical touch showed touch can significantly strengthen wellness in many ways, such as relieving stress, increasing attentiveness, improving mood, decreasing depression, enhancing immune function, lowering blood pressure, and relieving pain.

You can experience awe through touch in many ways, including taking a hot bath, getting a massage, tousling the hair of someone you love, feeling the sun on your face, eating chocolate that melts in your mouth, sleeping on a freshly made bed, walking barefoot on the ground, and more.

Try these ideas for developing your sense of touch to experience more awe:

1. Hold hands with someone you love for at least a few minutes (perhaps while taking a walk together). Then discuss how loving touch broke down barriers between you and gave you a fresh appreciation for each other.
2. Enjoy some uninterrupted time petting an animal and savoring the pure unconditional love that animal gives you through the sense of touch.
3. Spend some time walking barefoot through your home. Pay attention to the sensations you feel as you do so—from soft, bumpy carpet to cold, smooth floors.

## DISCOVER SPIRITUAL WONDER THROUGH OUR PHYSICAL SENSES

Our senses can be powerful portals to awe. The Bible celebrates the spiritual value of our physical senses in many verses, such as Proverbs 20:12 ("Ears that hear and eyes that see—the LORD has made them both.") and Psalm 34:8 ("Taste and see that the LORD is good; blessed is the one who takes refuge in him."). As we pay attention to our physical senses, we can discover spiritual insights that lead us to wonder.

## QUESTIONS TO PONDER FOR WONDER

1. Look at yourself in a mirror. Do you like the person you see? Ask God to help you see yourself as he sees you—someone who is loved and valuable. What is one change you can make in your life to help you live with greater confidence in the beauty of your soul?
2. What kinds of music do you like to hear? Do you create music by playing an instrument or singing? How can you use the power of music to experience more wonder in your daily life?
3. Think about your favorite scents. What memories do they trigger for you? How can you use a fragrance you enjoy to create a new and memorable experience of wonder?
4. Have you gotten stuck in a rut with your meals and snacks? How can you break out of your routine to try new foods, drinks, and recipes?

5. Are you getting the amount of loving touch you crave from day to day? How can you give the gift of loving touch—from handshakes to hugs—to others who need encouragement?

# Chapter 6

## Manage Time Well

The sound of loud cheering erupted outside my office window as I edited a magazine article. *It's here already.* Panic arose within me. The Olympic flame was scheduled to pass right by my office in Alexandria, Virginia, before the 1996 Summer Olympics in Atlanta, Georgia. My colleagues and I in the editorial department of The Salvation Army's USA headquarters eagerly anticipated seeing the iconic flame together. We planned to meet outside our building beside the Mount Vernon Trail, where the relay runners would carry the torch southward on its inspirational journey. When the time came for us to step away from our desks and head outside, I told the group I'd join them soon, thinking I had plenty of time to finish rewriting a few paragraphs.

The cheering happening now meant I'd miscalculated the time. Rushing to the window, I saw neither torch nor runners. I ran outside to the trail as fast as I could in high heels and a dress, frantically trying to see the flame in the distance—but the runner was already too far away to be visible. Wonder had literally passed me by.

Since then, determined to avoid more Olympic regrets, I've made time to watch and enjoy every summer and winter Olympics as fully as possible on television. Tumbling gymnasts, racing swimmers, and jumping volleyball players have captivated me during the summer games. Speeding skiers, dancing ice skaters, and spinning snowboarders have mesmerized me during the winter games. I've savored the beautiful pageantry of Olympic opening and closing ceremonies. Stories of people around the world rising beyond national conflicts to embrace mutual friendships at the Olympics have inspired me. Many moments of wonder have come into my life since I've scheduled time to watch the games when they're broadcast. I'm pulled into the present moment every time I experience a powerful moment of awe in the Olympics. I'm not concerned about the past or the future when I'm watching Olympians in action. All that matters to me is what's happening right now, because it's so wonderful.

Wonder has the power to change our perception of time and frees us to be fully present. Our regrets about the past and worries about the future fall away like broken chains. During awe-inspiring experiences, we focus on enjoying and learning from what's happening now. In the process, time expands in our minds.

Researchers have found that feeling awe changes how people perceive time, and in the process their well-being becomes stronger. A study[1] showed people experienced time much differently when they felt awe than they did when not feeling transcendent emotions. They reported they had more time available than they had thought they did. They said they felt more patient, more motivated to volunteer their time to help others, and more attracted to spending time on experiences rather than pursuing material products. Participants also reported feeling greater life satisfaction in general during times when they felt wonder. These effects on health and decision-making result from awe's ability to slow down time for people, the study found.

Experiences of wonder direct people's attention to the present moment. When they're fully present, their perception of time changes, their decisions change as a result, and their overall life satisfaction increases. They're less rushed, and the lack of stress about time helps them pay full attention to awe.

Several previous research studies have found that awe-inspiring experiences often make people feel a sense of timelessness in the present moment. Those studies explored various types of wonder—nature experiences in the wilderness,[2] athletic experiences,[3] and spiritual experiences.[4]

## MAKE WONDER A HIGH PRIORITY

Wonder constantly knocks on the doors of our lives. Yet too often, we don't notice because we're simply not paying attention. We can miss countless wonderful experiences by keeping ourselves so busy we're too exhausted or distracted to notice the awe around us. We must learn how to prioritize wonder while managing our time. We must not let the demands of our daily tasks take over our schedules and feel like that's the most responsible choice. We significantly limit our quality of life when we limit our focus only to our tasks without looking beyond them for greater meaning.

Chores and errands aren't enough in themselves to inspire us. Our souls crave the wonder we can find by living intentionally, even while doing mundane tasks. When we neglect making time for awe, we neglect our souls—the core and most important part of ourselves. Ultimately, it won't matter if we've caught up on our laundry or cleared our email inboxes. The time we've spent with wonder grows our souls, which live forever.

# Wake Up to Wonder

We can settle for living in shells of stress and settle for occasional glimpses of awe whenever we happen to notice it break through those shells. Or we can intentionally choose to make pursuing wonder a high priority day by day. That starts with getting rid of the excuses we've used in the past to tell ourselves awe isn't worth spending time pursuing. Here are the two most common excuses for not making time for wonder:

*The "irresponsible" excuse says:* Wonder is nice, but not necessary. I enjoy being surprised by awe, but I'm not going to make time to look for it. I have more important, more serious responsibilities. I might get distracted from everything else I have to do if I let myself make more time for wonder. I want more awe in my life, but I'm not a kid anymore. Chasing wonder doesn't seem responsible.

*The "impractical" excuse says:* Sure, I would love to pursue more wonder in my life if it were more practical to do so. Sometimes, I think about doing something awe-inspiring— like buying tickets for a concert or visiting a park—but I don't follow through because those plans are impractical. I have limited time, energy, and money. I'm afraid I won't have enough resources left for more practical pursuits if I let myself chase after experiences of wonder.

Experiencing awe on a regular basis is essential to living well. There is no valid excuse for denying yourself the gift of wonder God gives you every day. Awe may sometimes feel frivolous because it's fun, but it has a very serious purpose. Wonder shows you more about God and inspires you to move closer to him. There are many practical ways to incorporate awe into your life, and this book describes them, so you never have to worry about being impractical. No excuses.

Don't feel guilty about choosing to include wonder in your schedule whenever possible. Other people will have their own agendas for your time, but what matters most is how you believe God wants you to plan your schedule. Saying "no" to some commitments frees you to say "yes" to those that will help you experience awe. Saying "no" to others with respect and confidence is difficult, but once you establish the habit, you can enjoy wonder without looking back. Ask God to give you the courage to start doing so.

## PAY ATTENTION TO THE PRESENT

The Royal Observatory Greenwich in England keeps our planet's official time. Earth's twenty-four different time zones begin and end in Greenwich, at the prime meridian on the observatory's grounds. On an impulse, my family and I decided to take a ferry to Greenwich from downtown London one afternoon. Once there, we realized just how much there was to do at Greenwich. Seeing everything wasn't possible before we had to depart on the last ferry of the day. I ran up the observatory's steep hill, rushing past other tourists in my zeal to maximize my time at this famous timekeeping place. At the hilltop museum, I studied a map in an exhibit gallery full of time gadgets—from ancient sundials to current GPS satellite atomic clocks that can accurately measure nanoseconds.

I caught one of the many thoughts racing through my mind. I'd forgotten to make our family's dinner reservation for that evening. Panicking, I called the restaurant, and just then, Justin pointed out an interesting clock nearby. I carried on conversations with both a restaurant employee and Justin simultaneously while also scanning the museum map to plan the schedule.

Proud of myself for multitasking (even though research shows that multitasking *decreases* productivity[5]), I was humbled by what happened next. A grandfather clock startled me with loud chimes, I dropped the map, and while stooping down to pick it up, I mistakenly hung up before completing the restaurant reservation. An announcement came over a loudspeaker for a planetarium show that was about to start—another activity I wanted to cram into our busy afternoon.

The sounds of the clocks ticking around me seemed to echo the time stress in my mind. Overwhelmed, I remained kneeling on the floor where I'd dropped the map, hyperventilating. Justin touched my shoulder. "Are you okay, Mom? Can you breathe?"

*Breathe.* I nodded and slowly stood up. I focused on my breathing to try to calm down. As I inhaled and exhaled, gradually my awareness of God's constant presence with me increased and my stress level decreased. Well-being research shows paying attention to breathing in the present moment—a key part of mindful meditation, called mindful breathing—sharpens mental focus. A study[6] found that people were able to make wiser choices after fifteen minutes of mindful breathing. My perspective changed in just a moment or two while I breathed mindfully. As I inhaled and exhaled, the peace only God can give settled within my soul. I remembered time is relative. Time is nothing more than a way for people to measure change from different reference points. However, God is eternal.

Wonder is as close to us as our next breath, because God is always present with us, and we can become aware of his presence through the Holy Spirit's inspiration. Jesus compares the Holy Spirit to the wind in John 3:8 and sends the Spirit to his disciples by blowing on them in John 20:22.

The Spirit inspires us when we seek God. The root of the word "inspire" is the Latin word "inspirare" meaning "to breathe or blow into or upon," according to the Merriam-Webster dictionary, eleventh edition. That is reminiscent of God breathing life into the first human beings. Breathing is a simple, yet sacred tool God has given us to connect with his wisdom anytime.

After that mindful breathing encounter with the Holy Spirit at Greenwich, I was able to enjoy awe from a few brief museum activities without worrying about what I missed. That was possible by embracing each moment as a simple yet profound gift from God.

## WELCOME SCHEDULE INTERRUPTIONS

The day after a severe overnight thunderstorm, Honor and I were walking through our neighborhood when we spotted three baby robins and a nest on a sidewalk. The nest had apparently fallen from the tree during the storm. Two of the birds were dead, but one was loudly peeping as if sounding an alarm call of distress. Honor wanted to help that little robin, but I hesitated. What would helping an injured bird require? How much time would it take? My long to-do list flashed through my mind. I didn't want to interrupt my schedule to figure out how to help the injured (and likely orphaned) robin, thinking cynically the poor creature would probably die soon anyway. The robin was persistent, peeping at us and staring us down. "Please, Mom?" Honor asked. Her repeated "please" several times over the sound of the bird's "peep" was like beautiful music that touched my heart. Yes, helping would be inconvenient and perhaps useless, but I knew I shouldn't walk away from that robin.

We rushed back home, where I called our local animal control office for advice. A wildlife rehabilitator who works with birds was available to come into the animal shelter to treat the bird—if we could transport the tiny creature there. As I wrote down a long and detailed list of instructions for how to pick up and transport the robin, I realized I'd have to cancel the rest of my plans for that day. Waiting for a more convenient time wouldn't work because the robin needed help right away to survive.

The simple choice to allow the interruption in my schedule led to all sorts of wonder.

I shared a mother-daughter adventure with Honor. Watching her care for the robin with gentleness and a meticulous attention to detail challenged me to be more caring and patient myself.

I learned facts about American robins that made me feel awe. They love to sing in choruses, they migrate thousands of miles each year, and they build close social relationships with each other.

I got to know some wonderful people who contributed to the process of helping the little bird. One was a next-door neighbor, Cathy, who I hadn't gotten to know before. That changed when she came over to our yard while Honor and I were trying to put the little bird into a box. Cathy offered to loan us a much sturdier carrier. We learned Cathy ran an animal rescue organization that helped thousands of cats and dogs every year. Later, Honor volunteered there.

Ultimately, the robin recovered well, and the wildlife rehabilitator released the bird back into the wild. I'll always be grateful for the wonder that little bird brought into my life through a simple interruption.

When we choose to see interruptions as opportunities rather than as inconveniences, we can start noticing all the awe that comes into our lives unexpectedly. Often, wonder comes to us through unexpected opportunities to serve.

God wants us all to be on call for whatever comes our way, willing to help people even when their needs interrupt our plans. In Luke 10:25–37, Jesus told the parable of the good Samaritan who interrupted his journey to help an injured man, even though doing so cost him valuable time and money. God wants us to make ourselves available too. If someone's genuine need for help interrupts our plans, and we sense God leading us to act, we may be dealing with a divine appointment. Responding to divine appointments helps us see what has eternal value, which helps us perceive the awe around us.

## LIVE IN SYNC WITH NATURAL RHYTHMS

Stepping outside my home office on a Sunday afternoon, I walked away from the temptation of working on the Sabbath. I had spent too many Sundays after church sneaking in work I didn't really need to do on weekends. Yet, I craved the buzz of constantly feeling productive and important because of it. Leaving the house entirely would help me overcome my craving for that feeling. Rain came down in a steady downpour outside, so I slipped on some boots and grabbed an umbrella for a wonder walk.

As the rain purified the air around me, I breathed in the fresh scent. Water droplets blew under my umbrella, refreshing my skin with their gentle touch. The grass and soil I walked across soaked up rainwater like they were grateful for the gift. While countless raindrops fell from the sky, I felt as if God was sending grace down from heaven. James 4:8 came to mind: "Come near to God and he will come near to you. Wash your hands, you sinners, and purify your hearts, you double-minded." I said a spontaneous prayer, committing to choose God over work and keep the Sabbath holy *every* week. God's presence felt tangible, saturating my soul like rain. Washed clean of my self-imposed pressure to work every day, I could enjoy the wonder of soaking in God's unconditional love. I splashed in puddles, danced in circles, and caught raindrops in my mouth—unworried by how much time I spent enjoying it.

The Sabbath is a gift from God, although it may seem like a burdensome obligation at first. This weekly day of rest and worship is meant to help us live in a healthy rhythm rather than struggling against the natural rhythms of creation. Observing a weekly Sabbath day clears away stress so you can experience much more wonder than you could otherwise. This supports the well-being of both your body and soul, empowering you to be optimally receptive to awe. If you must work on Sunday, you can observe the Sabbath on another day.

God urges us to accept his offer in Matthew 11:28: "Come to me, all you who are weary and burdened, and I will give you rest." Observing the Sabbath will plug us into a rhythm of rest that naturally works best for us.

There is a greater purpose to our time than simply being productive. By tuning into life's natural rhythms, we can see glimpses of that overarching purpose—the great story written by God, in which we all play important parts—and encounter awe in the process.

Enjoying the four seasons God has nature rotate through each year can also connect us with wonder. Each season offers transcendent experiences which are only available during that particular time. We can learn from the beauty of each season by reflecting on its distinctive symbolism.

*Spring symbolizes renewal.* Spring is the time when nature wakes up for another year with many signs of hope—

from blooming flowers to the birth of new animals. I visit gardens each spring, and I also visit a farm to play with baby animals. Too often, we adults feel embarrassed about still enjoying some of the activities we enjoyed as children. I'm not ashamed I still like to pet piglets, feed newborn lambs, and watch fuzzy ducklings waddle around. We can give ourselves permission to pursue whatever spring activities renew our souls with awe. Just as spring flowers emerge from the ground, we need to emerge from stress to thrive. Wonder helps us do so.

*Summer symbolizes vitality.* Summer is the time when plants and animals throughout the natural world are growing and exploring to the fullest. During the summer, adventures of wonder await us everywhere in nature. I love being outside on summer evenings, when my neighborhood transforms into a wonderland. The sound of buzzing crickets pulsates from trees, different types of fireflies flicker their white or yellow lights, and the sweet fragrance of honeysuckle flowers fills the air. No matter where you live, summer is a season to enjoy the outdoors – a beach, forest, or any other wild landscape. The vitality of the natural world that God has created can renew your strength as you soak in the wonder of it. All of nature reflects something about God. Exploring nature during summer can inspire you to find rest and rejuvenation in a relationship with the One who created it all.

*Fall symbolizes wisdom.* Fall is the time of bounty and evaluation, as farmers harvest crops and animals take stock of their food. My family and I celebrate the bounty of fall every year by trying out different varieties of apples. We search for exotic varieties at markets in our area and visit local apple orchards to pick our own. Each new type of apple we discover gives us a new sense of wonder for its Creator. You probably know the most popular apple varieties (such as Honeycrisp, Red Delicious, Fuji, and Granny Smith) well. However, there are more than 7,500 different kinds of apples. Here are just a few exotic apples to try—Glockenapfel (bell-shaped), Custard Apple (bumpy skin that looks quilted), Pink Pearl (pink flesh), Elstar (tastes like honey), Stayman Winesap (tastes like wine), and Hawaiian Mountain Apple (tastes like rose petals). The autumn harvest highlights the wondrous variety of food God has given us. We can use the fall season to evaluate our choices in life and ask God for the wisdom to make the best choices.

*Winter symbolizes contemplation.* Winter is the time when much of the natural world becomes dormant, with plants resting and some animals hibernating. During winter, I continue my daily practice of walking for wonder, and I especially enjoy walking over snow. There's something profoundly peaceful about snow. Snow slows life down, disrupting our busy schedules by closing our schools and offices while motivating us to pay attention to the natural world it covers like a calming blanket. Snow whispers to our souls that we should pause to reflect on our lives. Even if it doesn't snow where you live, you can still benefit from winter's calming effect by walking outside in the cool air among bare trees. I've encountered great inspiration from praying and meditating while walking.

If we build our schedules around chasing to-do list items, we'll fall into a blur of busyness. Some awe can break through to us when we rush from one activity to another, but most will pass us by unless we align our schedules with natural rhythms. We can still feel important when we dare to stop dancing to the frenetic rhythms of maximum productivity during the day and exhaustion at night. God invites us to dance in sync with the natural rhythms he has designed—the hours of each day and night, the weekly Sabbath rest, and the seasons of each year. When we do, we can fully experience the wonder around us.

## MAKE A HABIT OF PURSUING WONDER

We can expect to find wonder anytime and anywhere when we regularly make time to pursue closer relationships with God. God may communicate to us in a myriad of ways. The closer our relationships to God become, the more his Holy Spirit will work through our lives, inspiring awe in us. As Daniel 4:3 declares, "How great are his signs, how mighty his wonders! His kingdom is an eternal kingdom; his dominion endures from generation to generation." We can confidently expect to experience wonder on a regular basis as we walk with God through life.

## QUESTIONS TO PONDER FOR WONDER

1. What excuses prevent you from making wonder a high priority in your schedule—and how can you overcome them?
2. How do thoughts about the past or future distract you? What could you do to start living more in the present, fully aware and appreciative of each moment of wonder you experience?
3. There are many ways to practice mindfulness. Which ways are some of your favorites, and why? What is one new mindfulness practice you can try to help you manage your time well?
4. What interrupted you lately in a way that led to wonder? What would help you say "yes" to the next divine interruption you encounter?

5. How can you live in better sync with natural rhythms—the daily hours, the weekly Sabbath, and the seasons—to experience the wonder of those special times?

# Chapter 7

## Enjoy Nature

Stepping out of a rustic cabin in Yellowstone National Park, I came face to face with a bison standing on the porch. The bison turned his head in my direction as I gasped in surprise. We stared at each other for a few long moments. Would the massive creature charge at me? My heart began racing. As I studied the bison's muddy brown eyes, however, I saw reassuring gentleness and curiosity. Then the animal shuffled off the porch and began grazing in a nearby meadow dotted with vibrantly colored wildflowers. I followed him from a safe distance and watched with wonder as the summer sun shone down. While the bison munched on grass, I munched on a granola bar, grateful for the Creator's simple gifts. A breeze blew around us, ruffling my wavy blonde hair, the bison's wiry brown fur, and the tiny green blades of grass on which we stood. Immersed in nature, I felt the presence of God, who had created it all.

Every part of nature displays evidence of God's work. While we don't see God's spirit physically in our earthly dimension, we do see his qualities reflected in nature. The Bible directs those who want to know the Creator to look for him in the natural world. "For what may be known about God is plain to them, because God has made it plain to them. For since the creation of the world God's invisible qualities—his eternal power and divine nature—have been clearly seen, being understood from what has been made, so that people are without excuse" (Romans 1:19–20).

A research study[1] of wilderness therapy programs found people who engage with nature are happier and healthier than those who don't. The reason? Experiencing the wonder of nature inspires people to feel awe, which then strengthens their well-being. Another study[2] found that enjoying nature seems to benefit well-being by inspiring people to feel connected to something beyond themselves. That feeling may include becoming more aware of God's presence with them.

One afternoon at work, I slumped down in my desk chair, clicking between many different computer screen tabs. I chose one and tried to focus on the task, but my mind was too frazzled to concentrate. I took a wonder break in nature and immediately felt better. Clouds drifted gently through a wide-open sky. Gazing at the simple natural scene reminded me I'm surrounded by a world that is greater than the stress in each day. Circumstances change like passing clouds, but the Creator's strength is always there to rely upon. I stood there for a minute or two, soaking in nature. Then I returned to my desk energized and finished the workday with optimal productivity.

An analysis of more than one hundred forty research studies linking nature to well-being[3] shows that spending time outside has significant and diverse benefits. One of those benefits is less stress, as I experienced on that workday. Other benefits include less risk of many diseases (from heart disease to type II diabetes), better sleep, and even a longer life.

Whenever we're immersed in the wonder of nature, we're in an environment God has specifically designed for our good. Nature reminds us we have a wise and loving Creator who sustains all of creation—including us—in powerful ways. Every part of nature can reveal something awe-inspiring to us about God's character.

Let's explore how five aspects of nature commonly found around the world—the sun, water, rocks, trees, and flowers—reflect God's glory.

## DISCOVER WONDER IN THE SUN

I woke up as beams of golden sunlight streamed through a window. The bright light dispelled the darkness of the previous night. An argument with a family member had left me feeling stressed. Dark thoughts about the conflict filled my mind as I ruminated about it. Finally, I entrusted the situation to God in prayer and fell asleep. The sun dispelled my darkness as it welcomed me to the gift of a new day. Lamentations 3:22–23 came to mind: "The steadfast love of the Lord never ceases; his mercies never come to an end; they are new every morning; great is your faithfulness."

The sun beams hope into our lives by reminding us we can draw strength from God's light day by day. Each morning, the sun reliably rises, sustaining life on earth in many vital ways—from photosynthesis (plants use energy from sunlight to produce food and oxygen for us) to heat (the sun's energy fuels weather patterns throughout our planet). Our world would literally fall apart without the sun. The force of the sun's gravity holds our earth and everything else in our solar system together in orbit.

Research shows sunlight is essential for our well-being. Health benefits from enjoying the sun's rays outdoors can include an immune system boost, better sleep, relief from depression, and stronger bones.[4]

As the natural light that sustains us, the sun reveals God's nature as the ultimate light. God's fiery, passionate love motivates him to give us life and sustain our lives. The Bible calls God the "sun of righteousness" in Malachi 4:2, "true light" in John 1:9, "light of the world" in John 8:12, "consuming fire" in Deuteronomy 4:24 and Heb. 12:29, "refiner's fire" in Malachi 3:2, and "bright morning star" in Revelation 22:16.

Sunlight is a symbol of life that comes from a loving Creator who cares for creation. Just as all living things on earth need sunlight to grow physically, people need the light of loving relationships with God to grow spiritually. Saint Francis of Assisi wrote a famous prayer praising God for the sun and its light:

> Be praised, my Lord
> For all your creatures
> And first for brother sun
> Who makes the day bright and luminous.
> He is beautiful and radiant.
> With great splendor
> He is the image of You, Most high.[5]

The sun also highlights how God enlightens us with wisdom to know the truth and make the best choices. Second Corinthians 4:6 connects light with wisdom, declaring that God "made his light shine in our hearts to give us the light of the knowledge of God's glory displayed in the face of Christ." In John 8:12, Jesus says he is the source of enlightenment: "'I am the light of the world. Whoever follows me will never walk in darkness but will have the light of life.'"

Finally, the sun sheds light on how God shines hope into the darkness of this fallen world. Ephesians 1:18–19 uses light imagery when describing the hope God offers:

"I pray that the eyes of your heart may be enlightened in order that you may know the hope to which he has called you." Physically, light always overpowers darkness. The photons in light can dispel darkness, but darkness cannot dispel light. This principle can be seen simply by entering a dark room and turning on a flashlight there. The light will be visible in the darkness, even if there's just a small amount of light in a great amount of darkness. This same principle applies spiritually, as the light of hope is always stronger than the darkness of discouragement and despair. No matter how dark our circumstances are, God can change them for the better by shining his light of hope into our lives.

## Discover Wonder in Water

The trickling sounds of water flowing through ice walls surrounded me as I walked through an ice tunnel. While navigating the slippery ice deep inside Iceland's massive Langjökull glacier, each step with the crampons on my hiking boots drew my attention to frozen water. The tunnel widened to reveal a room carved out of the glacier's strong internal ice—a chapel. Our group paused there to reflect on the wonder we were experiencing, and I sent a prayer of thanks to God. Our guide asked us to sing a simple song along with him, to hear the echoes of our voices against the chapel's frozen walls. As we sang together, our exhaled breath came out of our mouths in another form of water— steam—swirling among us in a white mist.

Water flowed freely both inside and outside of us. In that moment of awe, everything blocking my awareness of God's presence drained away. Water clarified the wonderful truth that I lived because of God's care, which constantly flowed through my life.

Water splashes God's life-giving role into our focus. In John 4:10, Jesus uses the term "living water" to declare his role as the world's Savior. A few verses later, Jesus uses the imagery of water to describe his gift of salvation: "but whoever drinks the water I give them will never thirst. Indeed, the water I give them will become in them a spring of water welling up to eternal life." (John 4:14). God gives us life, sustains our lives, and renews us. Water, which is essential for our bodies to live and thrive, reveals those qualities about God to our souls.

Water is constantly moving around our planet through natural cycles such as precipitation; evaporation; freezing, melting; currents in oceans, rivers, and lakes; the flow of groundwater, etc. God is constantly moving in our lives, often unseen but always at work. Water contains awesome power that people tap into for hydropower energy, which reminds us of God's even greater power to transform our lives.

Water, which has reflective qualities, also shows how the Holy Spirit counsels us with wise guidance. God does so when we reflect on our lives and ask for his help to live well. Water symbolizes clarity and purity and inspires us to look clearly at our lives and purify them by working with God for positive change to happen. I'm fascinated with the wonder of what the late researcher Masaru Emoto and his team discovered about water. Their pioneering experiments and photographs[6] found that water molecules form orderly, beautiful crystals when the water is exposed to positive words (such as prayer) expressed by people. When exposed to negative words from people (like hateful messages), however, water either forms chaotic, ugly crystals or fails to form any crystals at all.

Finally, water symbolizes God's great mercy toward us. Just as water cleanses our bodies from dirt, God cleanses our souls from sin. The ancient sacrament of baptism in water shows this. As people immerse themselves underwater, they accept God's forgiveness and let their sins wash away. As they rise from the water, they celebrate God's salvation gift through Christ, made possible by his resurrection.

## DISCOVER WONDER IN ROCKS

Several teenagers sat atop a boulder on the grounds of my neighborhood high school. They talked and laughed together as they swung their legs over the large rock's brightly colored face. Nearby, some other teens were opening paint cans preparing to repaint this community touchstone. Year after year, the boulder stood with reliable strength near the school's entrance. Students gathered there often. They frequently painted the rock with messages expressing their collective thoughts and feelings—from mourning (a suicide prevention message after a student killed himself) to celebrating (lauding the accomplishments of various award-winning student groups). They regularly took selfies at the rock, commemorating fleeting moments in their constantly changing lives at this rock-solid symbol of stability. They shared those selfies online, building a sense of community on the bedrock of their school experiences together.

Rocks, which are reliably strong, point to the fact God is trustworthy. The Bible calls God "rock" in First Corinthians 10:4, "living stone" in 1 Peter 2:4, and "cornerstone" in Isaiah 28:16.

Rocks also reflect God's eternal yet dynamic nature. The three different types of rocks on earth all have long-lasting durability yet are formed through dynamic processes. Metamorphic rocks come from intense heat and pressure, igneous rocks result from volcanic explosions, and sedimentary rocks form when layers of sediments compact together and harden. Rocks literally set the history of our planet in stone. After my first visit to the Grand Canyon—the most famous pile of rocks on earth—I wrote this poem:

A sea that once billowed deep and far has shrunk away
its waves now cast in stone.
Mountains sprouted and beckoned fire to the surface
in smoke and ash that blew away with the prairie wind.
A river slithered through
and cut its rage through soft earth
leaving jagged stone in tall, proud walls.
Now it seems the canyon rests.
At dusk its blues and grays and violets and indigos
meld into the sky like a curtain drawn upon a stage.
But deep in the black starless night
The Artist's hand is still at work.

The wonder of God's work is on display in every rock—from small pebbles at a creek to huge boulders on a mountain. Gemstone rocks called crystals display God's craftsmanship in special ways. Crystals are stunningly beautiful. Chapter 28 of the Book of Exodus describes how God instructed Moses to have the Hebrew people make a breastplate with twelve different gemstones. Each stone represented one of the twelve tribes of Israel and included crystals with beauty that people continue to admire today: amethyst, ruby, sapphire, emerald, topaz, turquoise, and more.

Any type of rock can inspire awe in us, which deepens our trust in God. As Deuteronomy 32:4 declares: "He is the Rock, his works are perfect, and all his ways are just. A faithful God who does no wrong, upright and just is he."

# Whitney Hopler

## Discover Wonder in Trees

Russ, Honor, Justin, and I connected to wonder when we placed our hands simultaneously on a sequoia tree's wide, bumpy trunk. Sequoia trees are the largest trees on earth. They may live more than three thousand years, growing to become more than two hundred fifty feet tall and more than thirty feet wide. Touching one of those ancient, gigantic trees—much greater than us physically—I rooted myself in the knowledge our family would be okay if we stayed connected to God. We had just emerged from the ordeal of Russ almost dying. This was our first vacation together in the aftermath of his lifesaving kidney transplant.

Many sequoias in the grove had survived devastating forest fires, just as we had survived the fiery stress of illness together. Some trees were still standing strong even though their massive trunks had been burned clear through. Not only had the sequoias survived; they had thrived. Sequoia trees welcome fire. The intense heat from fire bursts their cones open, releasing their seeds. Flames also clear the forest floor for those seeds to germinate, so these trees *need* to go through fire. Fire is a vital part of how they grow.

Our hands traced part of the charred black burn scar on the trunk of a sequoia. "I bet it hurt a lot when it got burned," Justin commented.

"But it's still here," Russ replied.

Justin hugged him, confessing his fear that his father's sickness meant he would leave us.

A park ranger told us that sequoia trees keep growing sapwood even after they get hurt by fire or some other type of trauma. Humans also keep growing after going through something hurtful. By simply being near a tree, we had found a greater perspective on our family's crisis. We were bound to face other challenges together. When we did, trees would remind us that challenges can help us grow.

Trees grow our perspective so we can understand more of God's wisdom and protection for us. In Jeremiah 33:15, the Bible predicts Jesus Christ coming to earth by using tree imagery. "In those days and at that time I will make a righteous Branch sprout from David's line; he will do what is just and right in the land." Trees stand tall as silent guardians of all around them. They can help us put roots into the solid ground of God's loving care for us.

Since trees stand in the same places for years, they may reflect God's constant presence in our lives. Some historical sites feature "witness trees," which have witnessed a memorable past event, kept growing, and still stand—inviting visitors to reflect on a location's history. I visited a witness tree called the Burnside Sycamore at Antietam National Battlefield in Maryland. A Civil War photographer captured an image of the tree just a few days after the tragic battle there. What struck me as I stood in front of the tree was how two main lower branches come together at its trunk. This tree stood in the middle of a massacre in 1862. Now it seems to symbolize peace between the two armies that fought each other on the Civil War's bloodiest day.

Trees remind us we're all a part of a greater story, connected to each other and to God.

We can experience awe even from spending just a brief time looking at trees. Participants in a research study,[7] who spent one minute gazing at a grove of eucalyptus trees, reported feeling more awe than another group of participants who gazed at a tall building for one minute. The people who focused on trees also showed more humility, empathy, and compassion than those who focused on the building, and were more likely to make ethical decisions. All of that resulted from just one minute of viewing trees.

A plethora of research studies[8] reveal the wonder which people experience from being around trees can strengthen every dimension of people's well-being. Mental advantages from being near trees include *less* anxiety, hostility, fatigue, sadness, and confusion, and *more* peace, energy, positive feelings, and concentration. Physical benefits include better breathing, better heart health, and a stronger immune system. Community benefits include less crime and stronger relationships.

Experiencing the wonder of trees can teach us valuable lessons when we make the time to learn them. Trees, which tower over us and exceed our lifespans, enlarge our perspective. They show we are each part of something much bigger than ourselves. We can look beyond our circumstances to God. Our personal stories are all connected to a greater story of what's happening on earth—the history of all us, traveling through time together. The Creator we all have in common has designed us to be closely connected to each other in relationships of love and respect. When we forget that, trees remind us.

## DISCOVER WONDER IN FLOWERS

Inside a flower-filled warehouse, Honor and I helped prepare a float for the Tournament of Roses parade, which is renowned for its natural floats featuring huge amounts of flowers. Even though our assignment didn't involve flowers—we crushed cocoa beans to use for an eagle's dark brown feathers—we marveled at the beauty of the flowers other volunteers were arranging. They carefully set roses, orchids, carnations, marigolds, daisies, and many more varieties of flowers into individual water vials.

Volunteers placed them into elaborate designs outlined in metal frames. Each flower had its own distinctive purpose in the grand design for each float, alongside other natural materials such as seeds and leaves. As millions of flowers found their places on the floats, they reminded me of God's orderly design for creation, where everyone and everything has a purpose. The more the individual parts of creation align with God's purpose for them, the more beautiful they can all become together.

When complete, the floats would only be used for a brief time—for the parade itself, and for a few display days afterward. Then workers would disassemble them and discard the flowers. Some flowers would be tossed in a compost pile. Others would be ground up into mulch. All flowers have short lives. They bloom briefly, only to decay soon afterward. God sees value in the wonder of every part of creation—even a lowly flower. The Bible compares people to flowers numerous times, and Luke 12:27–28 describes God's care for both. "Consider how the wild flowers grow. They do not labor or spin. Yet I tell you, not even Solomon in all his splendor was dressed like one of these. If that is how God clothes the grass of the field, which is here today, and tomorrow is thrown into the fire, how much more will he clothe you—you of little faith!"

Flowers make our minds blossom with an awareness of God's beauty. They showcase our Creator's lovely mix of orderly intelligence with fun, playful ideas. The wonder of flowers reminds us that God is the ultimate gardener. God formed the first human being out of soil (Genesis 2:7)—the same environment that nourishes flowers—and loves to see us grow and blossom. Jesus empowers that to happen when we're in relationship with him. He compares himself to a flowering plant (a vine) in John chapter 15 when he tells people, "I am the true vine and my father is the gardener" (v. 1) and "I am the vine; you are the branches. If you remain in me and I in you, you will bear much fruit; apart from me you can do nothing" (v. 5). Jesus was resurrected from a garden tomb, redeeming humanity's fall that had happened in the Garden of Eden.

Flowers are living reminders of the beauty of our Creator's love for creation, and the joy we can experience when we're lovingly connected to him.

Nature enlarges our perspective beyond the temporary concerns of our day-to-day lives. Its wild beauty resonates deep in our souls, reminding us a powerful Creator cares for us. Whether we're exploring woods, boating on a lake, or sniffing a rose, God will meet us there. Simply going outdoors in any natural setting can strengthen our awareness of God's presence.

## QUESTIONS TO PONDER FOR WONDER

1. What plans can you make to visit different types of natural landscapes (forests, mountains, lakes, deserts, beaches, etc.) to see the distinctive wonders they display?

2. What are some of your favorite qualities about God? How do certain aspects of nature (like the sun, water, rocks, trees, flowers, and more) help you reflect on those qualities and learn more about God? How can you incorporate more time in nature when you pray and meditate?

3. How can you schedule some natural wonder breaks in ways that renew your well-being when you're stressed or tired?

4. What fresh ideas do you need in your work and life right now? How can you seek inspiration from nature for those ideas?

5. How does wonder fuel your love for God the Creator and motivate you to care for creation? What are some specific ways you can commit to taking better care of our planet?

# Chapter 8

## Renew Your Mind, Part 1

The clear chrysalis hanging on a twig at a botanical garden slowly began to move. Inside, the orange, black, and white Monarch—which had just transformed from a caterpillar into a butterfly—wiggled its new body until the chrysalis opened at the bottom. Then the freshly changed creature slid out and stretched its new legs and wings. Complete metamorphosis is the scientific term for this transition. God's design empowers caterpillars to break down their bodies, releasing enzymes that dissolve almost all their body parts into a mushy substance rich in protein. The only parts of the caterpillars that haven't dissolved (cells that are called imaginal discs) use the mushy goo from the dissolved body parts to build a butterfly or moth body. The creature that emerges from the cocoon after this process is a different creature.

As human beings, we're all works in progress, changing and growing every day. We need to learn how to break down negative thoughts and build up positive thoughts. Our thoughts lead to our attitudes, which lead to our actions, which shape our entire lives in either positive or negative ways. Therefore, we need to choose positive thoughts that lead us to reaching our full potential. We'll encounter awe along the way.

Positivity promotes wonder by relieving stress, which makes it easier to pay attention to the wonder around us. Research shows choosing positive thinking can relieve stress in multiple ways, from feeling less distress in the moment to developing better coping skills during stressful situations.[1] The less stressed we are thanks to positive thinking, the more we can discover and appreciate the awe God ushers into our lives.

## RENEW YOUR MIND WITH THE HOLY SPIRIT

My friend Betsey's Bible study encouraged me to take her advice for dealing with my negative thoughts. A frustrating situation with some family members had triggered my bad habits of overanalyzing and worrying. The situation was out of my control. I kept ruminating despite my best efforts to ignore the problem. Betsey's teaching was always insightful, but today her message completely changed my perspective on the Holy Spirit. Connecting with the Spirit was possible anytime and anywhere, she said—not only in special circumstances. "It's as practical as breathing," Betsey told us. "Just as we constantly rely on our breathing physically, we can constantly rely on the Holy Spirit to help us spiritually."

I exhaled, imagining all negative thoughts blowing out of my mind and into the crisp fall air. I inhaled, silently praying for the Holy Spirit to blow positive thoughts in my direction. As I repeated the process for a few minutes, positive thoughts of peace and unconditional love toward my family members replaced the negativity I hadn't been able to remove on my own. Ever since then, I've often asked the Spirit to renew my mind. I've experienced the wonder of transformation every time. Romans 12:2 explains the importance of mind renewal. "Do not conform to the pattern of this world but be transformed by the renewing of your mind. Then you will be able to test and approve what God's will is—his good, pleasing and perfect will."

The Holy Spirit can help us develop a habit of positive thinking that leads us to awe. The Spirit does so by developing nine distinct positive attitudes in us when we cooperate with God's work in our lives. These are known as the "fruit of the Spirit" listed in Galatians 5:22–23: "But the fruit of Spirit is love, joy, peace, patience, kindness, goodness, faithfulness, gentleness, and self-control." As we pursue these attitudes, the Spirit will work in our minds, renewing them so we can perceive the messages God communicates to us. Let's look at how each fruit of the Spirit can lead us to wonder.

## DISCOVER WONDER THROUGH LOVE

"Turn to the person next to you and say, 'I love you,'" Lorna Byrne encouraged us at a weekend prayer retreat. My pulse began racing at the thought. I hadn't even said hello or made eye contact yet with the woman seated beside me, who was now embracing me in a spontaneous bear hug and saying she loved me. *How can she love me when she doesn't even know me? How can I love her when I don't even know her?*

Even as I struggled with shyness and anxiety, I wanted to accept the challenge. "I love you too," I said, returning the woman's embrace. Immediately, a warm feeling washed over me, as if simply saying those words had moved me closer to really expressing love.

Throughout the retreat, I got to know the woman, Tracy, and other retreat participants much more as Lorna gave us exercises to do together. The goal of every conversation or writing assignment was to grow in love. "God loves us all completely and unconditionally," said Lorna. She continued, "The best way we can grow spiritually is to learn how to love God, love ourselves, and love each other more."

On breaks, I watched Lorna, who is an introvert, like me, enthusiastically hug people and tell them, "I love you." No longer could I use my introverted temperament as an excuse to keep others at a distance. Once I decided to make the choice to approach every person I met with love, God gave me feelings of love for them—even for strangers and people whose actions or attitudes I didn't like. Each time that happened at the retreat, I thought of the biblical truth that every human being is a beloved soul made in God's image. Simply because of that, every single person on this earth is worthy of love.

Psalm 136:3–4 connects God's love with wonder: "Give thanks to the Lord of lords: *His love endures forever,* to him who alone does great wonders, *his love endures forever."* (emphasis added)

Research shows choosing love offers many benefits, including those that can help people experience awe, such as less anxiety, better stress management, and a happier life.[2]

1 John 4:8 makes the simple yet profound declaration "God is love." Since God's character is one of pure love, love is the foundation on which all the other fruit of the Spirit grow. Love leads us to joy by opening our hearts to embrace our relationships with God and each other. As we do so, we can develop the ability to experience joy. Joy taps into the well of our relationships (instead of our circumstances, like happiness does). So with the Holy Spirit's help, we can be joyful in any situation.

## Discover Wonder through Joy

On a cold gray winter day, I checked online for the official holidays celebrated on the second day of January and found two: World Introvert Day and National Buffet Day. I decided to eat alone at a local Indian buffet on my lunch break from work. Surrounded by the bright colors and pungent aromas of the food, my sadness about the end of the holiday season evaporated. Just because the day was not a major holiday like Christmas or New Year didn't mean there wasn't anything to celebrate. Every day of the calendar for the coming year noted a holiday to enjoy.

Some of the entries seemed wonderful to me: Step in a Puddle and Splash Your Friends Day (January 11th), Inventors Day (February 11th), Write Down Your Story Day (March 14th), Talk Like Shakespeare Day (April 23rd), Lost Sock Memorial Day (May 9th), Say Something Nice Day (June 1st), Creative Ice Cream Flavors Day (July 1st), Tell a Joke Day (August 16th), Dance Day (September 21st), Random Acts of Poetry Day (October 2nd), Play Monopoly Day (November 19th), and Pretend to be a Time Traveler Day (December 8th).

Other entries seemed so weird they were wonderful just for being funny: Big Wig Day (January 31st), Home Warranty Day (February 10th), Turkey Neck Soup Day (March 30th), Hairball Awareness Day (April 24th), Lumpy Rug Day (May 2nd), Axe Throwing Day (June 13th), Tape Measure Day (July 14th), Underwear Day (August 2nd), Be Late for Something Day (September 5th), Moldy Cheese Day (October 9th), Toilet Day (November 18th), and Pick a Pathologist Day (December 13th).

When we approach every day as a gift from God to enjoy, we can discover much more wonder than we can with a less positive mindset. A study found when people open their hearts to fully feel the emotional impact of joyful moments, they tend to notice the awe in those moments and respond with "wonder-joy tears."[3] Research also shows, conversely, experiencing awe can lead people to joy by improving their moods and increasing their life satisfaction.[4]

1 Peter 1:8–9 describes joy as a gift from Jesus Christ, which we can receive by choosing faith in him: "Though you have not seen him, you love him; and even though you do not see him now, you believe in him and are filled with an inexpressible and glorious joy, for you are receiving the end result of your faith, the salvation of your souls." Choosing joy leads to awe and shifts our focus away from our circumstances to God so we can experience wonder in any situation.

Research on joy shows it promotes awe in several key ways—relieving stress, improving decision making, and strengthening creative problem solving.[5] All those joy benefits help us notice and appreciate the wonder around us. A vital way to discover wonder through joy is to laugh. Humor opens our hearts and minds to consider situations from different perspectives, which leads us to awe. Research shows humor can be powerfully effective at relieving stress,[6] and when we're less stressed, we're more able to concentrate and notice the wonder around us. Other research reveals humor can promote creativity,[7] which helps us learn and discover more awe.

Joy leads us to peace by expanding our perspective so we can see more of how God is working in our lives. That perspective gives us the assurance we need to be at peace.

## DISCOVER WONDER THROUGH PEACE

My maternal grandmother, Nana, had a troubled look on her face as she lay dying. I leaned in closer to her bed to kiss her on the forehead. "You look worried, Nana," I said, clasping one of her shaking hands in mine. "What's on your mind?"

In a tremulous whisper, she replied, "There are things I wish I had done but didn't do. Now I've run out of time."

I squeezed her hand and sat in silence for a while, unsure of what to say. I could not give Nana more time to live—no matter how much I wished I could. Maybe I could help her find peace, though. "Nana, you know how I struggled with worry for years." She nodded. "Well, I've learned a habit that helps me. I visualize Jesus on the cross, and I visualize the specific things that are worrying me. Then I see myself walking toward Jesus and laying those things down at the foot of the cross for him to take care of for me. Through a short prayer, I ask Jesus for help with every specific thing I've left there for him. I see myself walk away then, and I always feel at peace afterward. Would you like for us to pray together that way about what's worrying you?"

Nana squeezed my hand with more strength than I knew she had. She nodded and closed her eyes. I prayed that Jesus would take care of every concern on her mind as she entrusted them to him. Then I asked Jesus to send her peace. I thanked him for his promise in John 14:27: "Peace I leave with you; my peace I give you. I do not give to you as the world gives. Do not let your hearts be troubled and do not be afraid."

During that prayer time together, the expression on Nana's face transformed from worried to peaceful.

Afterward, she simply said "Thanks" before falling asleep. She passed away the next day.

Peace is a wondrous gift from God. As we accept and open that gift day by day, we can discover awe. Americans from all religious backgrounds connect peace with wonder, research shows.[8] A Pew Research Center survey shows that 59 percent say they feel a deep sense of spiritual peace and well-being at least once per week, while 46 percent report feeling a deep sense of wonder about the universe at least weekly.[9]

The kind of peace God wants to bring to earth is known in Hebrew as "shalom" and means much more than the English word "peace" means. Shalom refers to complete well-being, with every part of creation existing in harmony with the Creator and thriving as a result. You can experience shalom within yourself, with other people, and with God.

Peace leads us to patience by giving us the confidence that every moment of our lives has real value. Even while we're waiting for something important, we can still be at peace because God is empowering us to accomplish good purposes day by day.

## Discover Wonder through Patience

Walking through a Walmart store with Honor when she was a little girl, I felt my shoes sink into something squishy. Lifting my feet to take more steps was no longer possible. A quick look down revealed both Honor and I had stepped right into the middle of a gray, gooey substance. Several large floor tiles had been removed in that area, and the sticky goo surrounded us where the floor was supposed to be.

"Mom," Honor said in a nervous voice, "I can't move."

"Neither can I," I replied. "Here, hold my hand and let's work together to lift our feet." Both of us strained hard to break our shoes free from the goo, but we remained stuck. I let go of Honor's hand as my pulse began to race and my hands started sweating.

"Oh my gosh, you all are stuck to the floor," said a woman whose face showed a mixture of amusement and concern as she stared at us. "I'll get help."

A small crowd of other customers gathered around us while we waited. Laughing awkwardly with them, Honor and I reached out to those who stretched out their arms for us to grab on—but they were too far away, and we stayed stuck.

A Walmart employee arrived, brandishing a bottle of rubbing alcohol. "If you pour this on your shoes, you should be able to step out of the adhesive," he announced. I caught the rubbing alcohol bottle he tossed to me. "Okay, just, um, pour some down the sides of your and your daughter's shoes?" he instructed with a tone of voice that sounded more like a question. "Hopefully that will work."

As I worked to loosen the goo's grip from our shoes, I heard an announcement over the store's speakers. "Whitney and Honor Hopler, please come to the customer service desk. Dayna Smith is waiting for you there."

"Oh, she's probably wondering what's taking us so long. We were supposed to meet her a while ago," Honor commented between giggles as I splashed more rubbing alcohol onto her athletic shoes.

"Well, I wish we *could* walk over there," I muttered. This unexpected delay didn't seem funny anymore, but I couldn't escape the irony of the situation. I had been in a hurry and rushing through the store with Honor, so I hadn't paid attention to where we were walking and ended up in this mess. I was also grateful to the customers and employees who waited with us, keeping us company while we stood stuck on the floor. They were a great group of people, and I never would have made time to strike up conversations with them if I was still rushing through the store.

Finally, our shoes lifted out of the goo, and we were able to escape from our ridiculous predicament by balancing on a chain of shopping carts and outstretched arms set up for us by the caring onlookers. As our shoes hit the floor tiles, cheers erupted from the crowd, and I found myself spontaneously hugging the people who had helped us. This wondrous moment happened because some people were willing to delay their own plans to help two strangers. Getting stuck that day, I realized, had been much more than just a stupid, annoying problem. The situation had been an opportunity to witness the wonder of compassion happening—thanks to patience.

Choosing to be patient can lead to awe in several vital ways, according to research.[10] Patient people feel more connected than impatient people do to our fellow humans and to God. That sense of connection helps them notice and enjoy wonder. Developing patience also helps people feel a sense of abundance in their lives that makes them hopeful and grateful, which can help them discover and appreciate wonder. Finally, those who are patient report experiencing stress relief and positive emotions that can lead them to awe.

Waiting isn't easy, living as we do in a society that promotes instant gratification. You may feel frustrated when you can't have something you long for right now. God may sometimes act more slowly than you wish he would to answer your prayers, since his perspective is eternal. People, with all their weaknesses, may often fail to meet your expectations. Therefore, patience is vital to have and put into practice.

As the Bible declares in Romans 8:25: "But if we hope for what we do not yet have, we wait for it patiently." You can't know when God will choose to answer your prayers, but you *can* count on the fact that waiting for his timing is always worthwhile. If you decide to trust God to act in his timing rather than trying to convince him to act in your timing, you'll eventually discover that God's answers will be better than you'd expected, because they'll come with his blessing.

Even though you do have to wait, you don't have to wait passively. The time you spend waiting can be much more than simply a boring and frustrating period to get through. In fact, you can be quite active while you wait, cooperating with God's work in your life. God has the best time in mind to answer your prayers. Waiting for God's answer in whatever situation you're facing is well worth the time—not only because God will ultimately respond, but because he'll change you in the process.

The ways God builds your faith while you're waiting are as important as the answer you're waiting. You can be confident the time you spend waiting isn't wasted, because God will deepen your faith in the process. So decide to follow the advice of Psalm 33:20–21: "We wait in hope for the Lord; he is our help and our shield. In him our hearts rejoice, for we trust in his holy name."

Patience leads us to kindness by helping us pay closer attention to the people around us. When we slow down enough to notice people, we can remember their value and become motivated to treat them kindly. We'll continue exploring the fruit of the Spirit in the next chapter, starting with kindness.

## QUESTIONS TO PONDER FOR WONDER

1. What negative thoughts do you struggle with now, which you would like to change moving forward? What positive thoughts would you like to make a habit of thinking about, and why?
2. How can you start relying on the Holy Spirit to help you love more day by day?
3. How can you start relying on the Holy Spirit to help you enjoy your life more day by day?
4. How can you start relying on the Holy Spirit to help you be at peace day by day?
5. How can you start relying on the Holy Spirit to help you be more patient day by day?

# Chapter 9
## Renew Your Mind, Part 2

Blowing just one short blast of his whistle in a precise tone, the shepherd led a group of border collie dogs to perform a series of complex actions. First, they surrounded a herd of sheep much larger than their own group. Then all the border collies assumed the same position, crouching low to the ground in a synchronized motion. Next, they stared at the sheep, and right then, the sheep responded by moving all together where the collies directed them—up a large hill, step by step, as the dogs opened up a path for the sheep to travel and the shepherd watched over them all carefully.

Watching this during a professional shepherd's demonstration, I thought of the words Jesus spoke in John 10:14, "I am the good shepherd; I know my sheep and my sheep know me." Until seeing an actual working shepherd working with his animals, I hadn't realized the depth of trust that's involved in the relationship between a shepherd and his flock. The more we trust our good shepherd Jesus, the more we can discover the best path to take in any situation, which leads us to experience more awe.

Day by day, we can discover more wisdom through the Holy Spirit's guidance. Jesus described the Spirit's teaching work to his disciples in John 14:26: "The Holy Spirit, whom the Father will send in my name, will teach you all things and will remind you of everything I have said to you." Cooperating with the Spirit's ongoing process of renewing our minds will keep leading us to awe, because we have a truly good God caring for us. When we trust him enough to rely on his loving care for us, we can look forward to him leading us to wonderful new adventures every day.

## DISCOVER WONDER THROUGH KINDNESS

Flipping through a stack of mail, I smiled when I saw an envelope from my friend Marilyn's address. I ripped open the envelope right away. Inside was one of her lovely handmade cards, with an even lovelier handwritten message inside. Marilyn poured out kind words in her poetic prose. They were exactly what I needed. A few days earlier, when we'd had lunch together, I'd shared a challenge I was going through, and she had spoken with kindness then. But now I'd received one of her "cards of comfort"—the cards she regularly makes and sends to people she knows need encouragement.

Whenever Marilyn writes kind messages, she taps into true spiritual power to bless each person who receives her cards. Marilyn's words aren't mere pleasantries. They are expressions of love in action—love that has made a powerfully positive difference in many people's lives. Only God knows how many people Marilyn's kindness has impacted through the years. Those who receive her cards often pay that kindness forward by encouraging others. Kindness is a wonder that keeps on giving.

Choosing kindness can help us notice the wonder around us by helping us focus more. Research shows kindness can increase energy and happiness while decreasing anxiety, depression, and stress,[1] all of which promote greater focus. Awe can also lead to kindness. Experiencing a sense of awe promotes kind feelings and actions by humbling people and helping them realize how connected they are to others, a study found.[2]

Our society celebrates "random acts of kindness" like giving directions to a stranger who's lost or buying a meal for a homeless person. To be most powerful, though, kindness should be more than just random acts. Kindness at its best is a consistent character trait we can develop. Colossians 3:12 urges us to respond to God's love by clothing ourselves with kindness. When kindness is something that distinguishes our character, we can enjoy the wonder of meaningful and lasting relationships.

Kindness leads us to goodness because we must open our hearts to be kind. Once we start a habit of open-hearted living, we're motivated toward good thoughts, words, and actions.

## DISCOVER WONDER THROUGH GOODNESS

Willie was much more than I'd expected him to be. A man who had been incarcerated since his youth—spending about forty years in prison—Willie had struggled with addictions to heroin and alcohol, which fueled his crimes. He had also struggled with anger, getting into frequent conflicts with his fellow inmates. One of those conflicts turned tragically violent. Willie got permanent scars on his body after inmates he'd been arguing with threw gasoline on his face and lit it. I suppressed a gasp when I first saw him, coughing instead to try to deflect his attention from my nervous reaction.

"Good to meet you," he said, extending one of his hands for me to shake.

Reluctantly, I did so, feeling the bumps of scars on his skin. The moment I shook his hand, guilt washed over me like a wave. Negative labels for Willie had swirled around in my mind as I'd fearfully prepared for this interview at the Salvation Army rehabilitation center where Willie lived—criminal, addict, offender, loser. I had harshly judged a man whom God had made—all before I'd even met him. Now, in Willie's presence, I saw he was a person with inherent worth that didn't depend on his past choices.

We started talking. Every word Willie said taught me something about forgiveness, courage, and trust. "When I looked at my face in the mirror after the attack, I knew I had a choice to make. I could choose to be bitter, or I could choose to be better." Willie's brown eyes shone with warmth as he talked. "That day I decided I would try saying a prayer."

Willie went on to describe how his life transformed as he took steps of trust that led him steadily closer to God. He told of relying on God instead of drugs and alcohol to cope with stress, pursuing truth rather than lying even when it was uncomfortable to do so, and opening his mind and heart to forgive himself and the people who had hurt him. Hearing Willie's wisdom transformed me, as well. My previous fear of Willie changed into something greater—respect. I learned we had more in common than I thought, like a silly sense of humor, and a love for jazz music. Where we differed, I saw I could learn from his perspective. Who was I to judge Willie for his past mistakes? That was God's job, not mine.

After the interview, I watched Willie light an Advent candle during a worship service at the rehab center. This was the first time he had been near fire since his face was burned in prison more than a year earlier. He struck a match with shaking hands and courageously lit the candle. In the glow, Willie's expression changed from apprehension to joy. The candlelight's reflection on Willie's smile revealed the light of hope God had shone into his life. We talked a bit more after the service, and Willie asked me to pray for him. I asked him to pray for me, as well.

Willie, I discovered, was truly a good man. His journey reminded me of Romans 12:21: "Do not be overcome by evil, but overcome evil with good."

Research shows choosing goodness can lead to wonder in ways that involve helping people focus more, which makes them more likely to discover and appreciate awe. Doing good decreases stress, increases happiness, and promotes mental health—all of which strengthen focus—according to research.[3] Wonder can also lead to goodness. When people experience awe from a spiritual experience, their brains change in ways that lead to goodness. Brain-mapping research reveals the area which establishes the sense of self in the world partially shuts down, while the area that controls emotions and arousal becomes more activated and releases dopamine (a chemical that causes people to feel good). As a result, people become more aware of their connection to others and more motivated to choose goodness.[4] Another study showed when people experience awe, they become motivated to do good through altruism.[5]

Being good can sometimes seem like an unrealistically lofty goal. After all, everyone struggles with the temptation to act in bad ways, and sometimes even good intentions don't lead to good behavior. But God isn't looking for legalistic "goody-two-shoes" people. He is a loving father who wants his children to be good, because he knows that's what best for them. Jesus declares in Matthew 7:12: "So in everything, do to others what you would have them to do you, for this sums up the Law and the Prophets." Doing the right thing is always within your reach if you rely on the

Holy Spirit's help. As you continue to make good choices, over time, God will transform you to become more and more like Jesus.

Goodness leads us to faithfulness because, to be good, we must rely on God's help. Relying on God challenges us to trust him for the help we need.

### Discover Wonder through Faithfulness

Looking out a window at home after a severe thunderstorm, I saw Dad's car navigating carefully between fallen tree branches in our street. I smiled and rushed to the door. My father reached our driveway, parked, and pulled out a bag full of freshly printed newspapers.

"What a storm that was," Dad said as he handed me the newspapers with a hug. "Is your power back on?"

"Not yet. How about yours?"

"Ours came back on about an hour ago. The *Washington Post* says that nearly everyone in our area lost electrical power last night." He pulled out that day's edition and flipped through it. "Here's an article with tips on how to keep the food in your fridge and freezer from spoiling while the power is out."

"Thanks, Dad."

My gratitude encompassed much more than thanks for that one day's newspaper delivery. I was really thanking my father for his faithfulness. Dad has a long history of delivering newspapers to family and friends every day, checking in with them personally about what's going on in their lives as well as in the world. So far, he has faithfully built community through his newspaper deliveries for more than seventy years. Now an octogenarian, the young Jim Wyckoff started delivering newspapers as a nine-year-old boy riding his bike around a delivery route to earn extra money after school. He discovered his neighbors often wanted to talk about the news in the papers. They would celebrate good news, share concerns about bad news, and laugh together about weird and wacky stories. Dad outgrew his delivery boy bike, started driving, gave up his afterschool paper route, and went to college. When he returned, he decided to start his own volunteer delivery route to stay in touch with loved ones. He began a faithful routine of buying stacks of newspapers at dawn and driving around our local area each morning to deliver them to people he wanted to check in with daily.

If folks aren't around to talk, my dad leaves their newspapers with a handwritten note like a care package. If they are, he gives each one a few minutes of his time. Of course today, people looking to be well-informed can get the news faster from electronic sources like TV and the internet than they can from print media like newspapers. Even Dad checks the news electronically now. But nothing can replace the pungent smell of newsprint, the crinkling sound of turning pages, or the black smudges of ink on our hands from newspapers. Reading newspapers is just a more tangible experience than perusing electronic news. Whenever my father hands a pile of papers to someone, the affection goes straight from Dad to them, as a special delivery.

My father has only had to take a few breaks from his newspaper deliveries, such as during the coronavirus pandemic lockdown. Most days, however, my dad shows up. Everyone on his delivery route knows they can count on him to be there for them.

Dad's faithfulness reminds me and my fellow newspaper recipients that we're all a valuable part of the greatest story of all—God's love at work in the world. As we stay in touch with what's going on in the world and with each other, God brings us together in love and uses us to make the world a better place.

All of us have God-given talents he wants us to develop and use. We also all have God-given purposes he wants us to discover and pursue. As we faithfully show up to do whatever we sense God leading us to do, we open doors for wonder to come into our lives.

Research shows faithfulness increases life satisfaction, which helps people appreciate awe. People who choose faithfulness report being more satisfied with their lives than those who don't. A study found those who gave faithful attention to their worship communities, their friendships, and their exercise routines said they felt fulfilled as a result. Their satisfaction increased as their faithfulness with those practices increased.[6]

Experiencing awe can also boost life satisfaction, motivating people to be faithful. A study revealed people who experience awe experience well-being as a result— due to their tendency to find meaning in their lives, and they are then motivated to engage in prosocial behaviors.[7]

You can always count on God to be faithful to you, even when you're not faithful to him. But your own faithfulness is important to God. You need to become a faithful person— someone who will stay close to God and reliably help other people. When you faithfully love God and others, you'll experience blessings yourself. "A faithful man will be richly blessed" promises Proverbs 28:20.

Faithfulness leads us to gentleness by keeping us closely connected to God, who is the ultimate example of gentle strength. God's essence of pure love inspires us and flows through us as we faithfully connect with him. We can be gentle as we tap into that love regularly.

## Discover Wonder through Gentleness

"I want to show you something," said Victor, a second-grade student at my children's elementary school, as he gently took my hand and led me over to his backpack. He pulled out a notebook and turned to a page featuring comic strip sketches. "In this story, the superheroes are talking, not fighting. They're talking about how to solve their problem instead of beating each other up. See?" Victor lifted the notebook toward me, and I quickly read his thoughtful work.

"This is great, Victor," I said. "I love it."

"Yeah? Really?" Victor looked at me with hope shining in his brown eyes.

"For sure." I smiled at him. "You have very good ideas."

I reflected on the first time I'd met Victor, when I saw him crying and asked him what was wrong. He told me some of his classmates had laughed at him during a class discussion about a cartoon. Victor had simply suggested that the cartoon characters talk about their conflict instead of hitting each other. Victor had opened up to me about how other students had called him names and excluded him from their groups on the playground because, he told me, "They think I'm weak, but I'm just trying to be gentleman, and my parents say that's a *good* thing."

Every time I saw Victor after that, I looked for ways to encourage him to see his gentleness as strength rather than weakness. As someone who had been teased relentlessly for my gentle nature while growing up, I had learned as an adult that gentleness was an asset. Many people—adults and children alike—opened up to me because they knew they could trust me to listen to them with care and respect.

"Victor, why don't you show this cool comic strip to your teacher and ask if you can share it with the class?" I suggested.

Beaming, Victor did so. When he presented his ideas in comic strip form, the students appreciated them. By the end of the school year, Victor had grown more confident—and thankfully, he was still just as much of a gentleman.

Practicing gentleness is vital to our ability to focus well so we can notice the wonder around us. Research shows gentleness is the key practice underlying the many "soft skills" (such as humility, compassion, respect, and listening) that help people pay attention and succeed at work.[8] Choosing to be gentle can lead to conversations that promote awe. As we talk gently about any topic together (even complicated, difficult, or emotional topics), we can learn from each other in the process.[9]

Jesus models gentleness as a sign of strength. He gives us a compelling picture of that in Matthew 21:5, where he chooses to enter Jerusalem as a king in a way that emphasizes gentle strength: "See, your king comes to you, gentle and riding on a donkey." In Matthew 11:29, Jesus encourages us to follow his example: "Take my yoke upon you and learn from me, for I am gentle and humble in heart, and you will find rest for your souls." Philippians 4:5 urges us: "Let your gentleness be evident to all. The Lord is near."

Gentleness can lead us to self-control by empowering us to control our strength and direct it in positive ways.

## DISCOVER WONDER THROUGH SELF-CONTROL

A woman looking down at her cell phone's screen suddenly collided with me as she rounded the corner of a bookshelf at the Library of Congress. The impact knocked my library books, notebook, and purse to the floor. A stinging pain started throbbing in my arm as I leaned against the bookshelf she had pushed me into. Glaring at the woman, I noticed her employee badge. She should be paying attention instead of talking on her cell phone during work, I thought with anger. Just as I opened my mouth to tell her off, I noticed something else—a caring expression on her face. I made eye contact with her, and that moment of connection inspired me to close my mouth. Instead of spewing out my anger in a lecture, I said a silent prayer for self-control.

"I'm so sorry," the woman said, picking up my fallen books. "Are you okay?"

I resisted the urge to complain and simply nodded.

"I was texting with a family member about an emergency and must have gotten distracted."

My self-righteous indignation dissipated with her words. "No worries," I heard myself say.

"Thanks." She held up one the books. "I see you're interested in classic movies and television. Are you going to the concert tonight?"

"What concert?"

"The Babalu concert in our Coolidge Auditorium to celebrate our Lucille Ball and Desi Arnaz collection."

"A concert in the *library*?" I'd always thought of libraries as quiet places, not concert venues.

"Yep—conga drums and all."

"I'd love to go, but I hadn't heard about it."

"Oh, that's too bad. The tickets have been gone for a long time. I bet I could get you a ticket if we have a last-minute cancellation, though. Consider the ticket a thank-you gift for being so gracious to me after I slammed into you like a runaway truck."

"Thank *you*," I replied, as excitement eclipsed all remnants of anger within me.

That evening, I sat in the front row as conga drums thundered onstage. Practicing self-control by defusing my anger had led to the librarian's kindness, which led me to a wondrous concert.

Research has found self-control benefits well-being in several ways that can lead to awe—increasing people's ability to focus, improving their relationships, and helping them learn.[10] Conversely, wonder can strengthen self-control. A study found experiencing feelings of awe helps people exercise more self-control by making it likelier for them to respond thoughtfully (rather than react on impulse) to situations.[11] Prayer can empower people to change the way they think, in ways that strengthen their self-control, according to research.[12]

1 Corinthians 10:23 describes the importance of self-control: "'I have the right to do anything,' you say—but not everything is beneficial. 'I have the right to do anything'— but not everything is constructive." Choosing to follow the Holy Spirit's guidance is the key to learning the self-control that can benefit us in many ways, including helping us experience awe. "You, my brothers and sisters, were called to be free. But do not use your freedom to indulge the flesh … walk by the Spirit." (Galatians 5:13, 16).

If you choose to think before you speak, exercise regularly, live free of debt, or even forgo an extra cookie at a party, you'll help others make healthy choices too. When you don't control your appetites for food, sex, money, or anything else, they begin to control you. Jesus can give you the power you need to master them.

As we cooperate with the Holy Spirit's work in our lives, we'll naturally wake up to the wonder around us. Hebrews

2:4 tells us God testifies to our salvation "by signs, wonders and various miracles, and by gifts of the Holy Spirit distributed according to his will." The closer we grow to God—the ultimate source of wonder—the more we can experience his gift.

## QUESTIONS TO PONDER FOR WONDER

1. How can you start relying on the Holy Spirit to help you be more kind day by day?
2. How can you start relying on the Holy Spirit to help you pursue more goodness day by day?
3. How can you start relying on the Holy Spirit to help you be more faithful day by day?
4. How can you start relying on the Holy Spirit to help you speak and act with more gentleness day by day?
5. How can you start relying on the Holy Spirit to help you practice more self-control day by day?

# Chapter 10

## Explore Mysteries

One May day while hiking in the Grand Canyon, I made all sorts of foolish mistakes: hiking alone without telling anyone where I was going, not bringing a cell phone, neglecting to plan how far to go and how much time it would take to return, and not carrying any snacks or enough water. On a whim of excited curiosity, I descended the Bright Angel Trail unprepared for its challenges.

I enjoyed the scenery and exchanged smiles with many other tourists while leisurely strolling along. A series of troubles started, though, when I met a group of people riding the canyon's famous mules. They were going up as I was going down. I had to flatten myself up against a canyon wall to make room for them to pass. As they did, one a mule let loose a copious amount of urine on my hiking boots. Every step I took after that assaulted my nose with a putrid smell. Not long afterward, I stumbled on a jagged rock and dropped my open water bottle. Dirt spilled inside when the bottle hit the ground, ruining what little water I had left. Still, I walked on, determined to see as much of the canyon as I could—without bothering to consider that pesky little problem of practicality.

As afternoon turned into early evening, no other hikers appeared on the trail. A glance at my watch alerted me more time had passed than I expected. A rumbling in my stomach reminded me of the restaurants up on the canyon rim. I reluctantly turned around and climbed against the force of gravity. In a dehydrated state, my legs began to feel like they had jelly inside.

I stumbled over a rock again. Teetering on the edge of the trail with one leg hanging off a steep cliff, I felt my mortality confronting me. Any wrong move could send me hurtling thousands of feet down into the canyon. Slowly and carefully, I crawled away from the cliff, sat down on the trail, and tried to cry. No tears came, though, due to my shock. As the sun started setting, I imagined becoming food for cougars after dark. "God, I'm going to need your help to get out of this canyon. Please!" I yelled into the air.

Humbled by reaching the end of my own abilities, I sat there unsure of what to do next as the sunset's light sent brilliant bursts of color onto the canyon's walls—pinks, oranges, and reds that were deeper than any hues I'd seen before. A breeze rustled around me, and I felt oddly peaceful.

A tall figure came into view, walking briskly up the trail. The figure appeared to be a man about seven feet tall, with wavy shoulder-length black hair and wearing a blue shirt and jean shorts. On every square inch of his body, it seemed, he was carrying camping equipment. A large backpack with a sleeping bag tied below it rode on his back. Cooking pots, containers, and various other types of gear clattered noisily as he walked with them strapped to his arms and legs like instruments in a one-man band. As I watched him, mesmerized, he stopped right in front of where I was sitting and peered down at me.

Face to face, I could see there was something extraordinary about the light in his intense blue eyes. Those eyes looked at me from his rugged, sunburned face like they knew me well, but I couldn't recall having ever met this man. Before I could think of what to say, he spoke.

"You can do it, Whitney," he said in a voice that told me this was no human being. His voice was like a lion roaring over the sound of thunder. It was an extraordinary sound. Words can't really do it justice. He spoke clearly, yet with such strength I felt the energy of his words roll over me like a wave. I wondered how he knew my name.

Then the man—who I now realized was an angel—grinned as if he knew my thoughts, as well. He nodded, and then turned to walk up the trail and out of sight, with all his camping equipment clattering away.

I sat there for a few moments, trying to absorb the encounter. Then I sprang to my feet with newfound energy. Somehow, I was able to hike up to the South Rim before darkness completely shrouded the canyon. I walked so fast that I nearly ran up the trail, even though I had been exhausted when I'd said my desperate prayer. After reaching the rim, I thanked God and then stared at the trailhead's sign, now barely readable in the fading light. Bright Angel Trail's name had new meaning for me. I had sought the wonder of nature on my own in foolish ways. What I discovered was wonder far beyond what I could imagine—wonder which only happened *after* I humbled myself.

We need to humble ourselves to be able to learn in ways that lead to awe. We must allow our assumptions to be challenged and our worldviews to expand. Who knows how much wonder we miss because pride blocks us from considering that a person or situation might have something valuable to teach us? Who knows how much wonder we can experience if we're humble enough to pay attention to mysteries that go beyond our own perspectives?

## GO BEYOND LIMITS

We welcome awe-inspiring mysteries into our lives by opening our minds to them, which sounds simple, but can be challenging. The reason is we can be disturbed by mysteries as much as we're attracted to them. Too often, we block ourselves from noticing and experiencing wonder because we're not open to something greater than ourselves. Encountering something greater means grappling with mysteries that call us to go beyond limits—beyond the limits of what we know, what we understand, and what we think is possible. Mysteries can be inspiring, terrifying, or somewhere in between to us—depending on how we respond to them.

Whether the mysteries we encounter seem negative or positive, we might ignore anything that doesn't fit into our comfort zone. We do so at our peril, because mysteries challenge us to evaluate and expand the ways we think and feel, opening doors for us to walk through to awe. We must be willing to explore mysteries if we want to wake up to wonder.

God designed us to be naturally curious, and mysteries play a vital part in how we express our curiosity. A team led by George Mason University researchers developed a curiosity scale, which showed two of the five main ways people express their curiosity relate significantly to how they respond to mysteries.[1]

One dimension of curiosity is "Joyful Exploration,"[2] which involves seeking new knowledge (including through mysteries) and enjoying the learning and growth that happens as a result. By seeking new information and reflecting on what they discover, people who express curiosity this way welcome mysteries, learn amazing insights from them, and appreciate that learning.

Another dimension is "Stress Tolerance,"[3] which involves the willingness to embrace the stress (such as doubt, confusion, and anxiety) that arises from exploring the mysterious (as well as what's new, unexpected, complex, or obscure). By choosing to explore mysteries despite the stress exploration can bring into their lives, people who approach curiosity in a Stress Tolerance way can also unleash amazing learning experiences as they express their curiosity.

In our society today, there are more ways for us to try to feel in control than ever before. We can search and find information for just about any topic nearly instantly online. All that easily accessible choice and knowledge can make us feel we can just dismiss the mysteries that make us feel uncomfortable.

We can track the status of package arrivals and pizza deliveries down to every detail. Do we really need to follow the journey of the items we ordered online as they make their way to us through various warehouses and shipping centers? Do we need to know that our pizza just entered the oven, or that it just came out, or that a team member is putting the pizza into a box at a certain precise moment of time? We can monitor every room in our homes when we're away, even though home robberies rarely happen, and our pets don't care if we're watching them from afar. We can use wearable devices to track all sorts of health data—physical activity, sleep, breathing, heart rate, blood sugar, sun exposure, and much more—yet are still vulnerable to becoming ill or injured.

Our technology gives us the illusion of control. Yet only God is truly in control. No matter how much we may feel in control of our lives, the fact remains we can be surprised by the unexpected at any time and place. God still can—and does—surprise us with mysteries.

## EXPLORE PUBLIC MYSTERIES

"What is that?" several people in our unidentified flying object (UFO) tour group exclaimed in unison as we stood in the Arizona desert, staring up into the sky. Our night vision goggles revealed glorious details beyond what humans can see with naked eyes—not just thousands of stars above us, but even the gasses burning on those stars. Our guide had directed our attention to a white light that wasn't behaving like a planet, star, or satellite. The light appeared to be moving at an extraordinarily fast speed and making sharp turns as it zigzagged through the sky. When we aimed our laser pointers in the light's direction, it seemed to respond to us by growing significantly larger and brighter—a behavior known as a "power up."

Was this mysterious light a UFO? Technically, the light seemed to meet the definition of an unidentified flying object, but what *kind* of object did we see? Theories abounded as we discussed the possibilities, from an alien spaceship to an angelic being of light. Could we believe the light was intelligent and interacting with us? After a few minutes, we aimed our lasers at it collectively once more—and again, the light powered up as if responding.

"Maybe it's watching over our planet," someone suggested.

"Maybe monitoring humanity," someone else said.

"If so, I wonder what it thinks of us goofballs down here on the ground?" another person responded.

What indeed? There was a pause long enough for us to ponder that question. Then we all broke out into raucous laughter.

In the back of my mind, however, I wondered whether there really could be some truth to UFO reports. There were so many of them, over so many years, in so many places around our planet. Also, our US government had spent millions of dollars to study UFOs.[4] High-ranking government officials such as former Senate Majority Leader Harry Reid went on record about what was known officially as the Advanced Aerospace Threat Identification Program, which had been partially declassified. The US Central Intelligence Agency (CIA) has released official documents related to UFOs, and the governments of many other nations around the world have declassified and released official documents relating to UFO reports and investigations.

The more I thought about what I'd just encountered, the more my mind opened to the possibility that non-human intelligent life was watching us. Considering that didn't have to be hard. After all, I believed in angels—light beings who are constantly going back and forth between dimensions. Anytime their vibration slowed enough to fall within the range of human vision, angels could appear as UFOs. It was realistic, as well, to expect that intelligent life existed on other planets throughout the universe. Many astronomers think some of the planets they've discovered so far are capable of sustaining life, and the sheer number of other planets in our vast universe makes it statistically likely that alien life exists. Even though I thought the UFO phenomenon was weird, it was a mystery worth considering. The wonder I'd experienced that night was too valuable for me to remain close-minded any longer.

People sometimes give UFOs credit for creating another mysterious phenomenon—crop circles. Researchers haven't pointed to a conclusive answer for why crop circles exist.[5] Yet they remain fascinated by the wonder of crop circles' designs. When people use the universal languages of mathematics and music to decode those designs, they can discover benevolent messages inside the symbols, such as taking good care of creation.[6]

Crop circles appear all over our planet, but many of them appear in a concentrated area of southern England that's also home to the famous ancient standing stones of Stonehenge and Avebury. Crop circle designs had fascinated me for years. Finally, I decided to travel to England to see if I could find some crop circles and experience firsthand what walking in one was like.

I found a crop circle that had appeared overnight recently in a wheat field. The circle, in the Hackpen Hill area of Wiltshire, featured a star inside a circle, surrounded by two more concentric circles. Perfect geometric proportions held the entire design together, following the Golden Ratio and Fibonacci sequences of numbers—mathematical patterns that occur in nature, from human DNA to flower petals.

Stepping inside the crop circle, I felt a tangible surge of energy that made my skin tingle. Was I experiencing the good vibes from high frequency electromagnetic energy, like researchers have measured inside some crop circles?[7] Or was I simply so excited to be there that my emotions had manifested physically? The further I walked into the field of wheat on that sunny July day, the more questions I had, even as my sense of wonder grew.

Still, an argument I heard outside the circle between two men distracted me. The driver I'd hired had confessed to me earlier he was a skeptic who suspected all crop circles were hoaxes. A crop circle researcher believed a force beyond humanity was creating most of the circles. Genuine crop circles, he argued, change the plants and the soil on which they form. Indeed, I'd read about lab tests showing the plants in some crop circles become significantly healthier at the cellular level, and the soil becomes magnetized.[8] Plants inside hoax crop circles are simply crushed and damaged. The researcher added that hoaxes feature imperfect measurements in contrast to the perfect proportions of genuine circles. The driver nodded, yet also smirked. "Maybe so," he replied. But if people hadn't created this crop circle, then who had? Aliens? Fairies? Leprechauns? Bigfoot? The possibilities seemed implausible to him.

I could identify with both men. My analytical personality and training in investigative journalism led me to be skeptical of what I might find there. Yet, I was also insatiably curious and in love with God, which led me to seek out inspiration and leave my mind and heart open to the possibility of discovering something truly wonderful in that wheat field.

As I walked, I stopped worrying about the loud debate going on between the driver and researcher and focused on the circle itself. The symbolism of the shapes suggested something about wholeness, eternity, and unity (the circles), as well as humanity and protection (the star). I couldn't be more precise than that, but I made peace with the tension of not really knowing.

Vibrant green and yellow stalks of young wheat plants carpeted the circle. Walking on them was like walking on a bouncy mat woven into complex patterns. I heard myself laugh with joy as I walked, overcome with the delight of pure wonder. Somehow, I felt connected to the circle—as deeply connected as if my own body was planted in the earth along with the wheat. A sense of awe for the beautiful order of God's creation filled my soul as I watched the birds flying overhead, listened to the people talking nearby, and felt the warm sunlight shining down on the field.

I reached out to brush some standing wheat stalks. They formed the raised shapes in this living work of art. My skin tingled with gentle pulses as I ran my hand through the stalks. That feeling delighted me with wonder.

After I emerged from the circle back into the "normal" landscape, I wondered about that awesome experience. The frustration of not being able to fully understand and explain what I'd experienced in the crop circle was stressful. But I didn't want to be able to shrink the experience down to whatever the answer was. The mystery was far more compelling.

Mysterious experiences in nature can be powerful access points for awe. People report being especially inspired by nature after spending time in natural settings that are mysterious, according to research.[9] Since encountering natural mysteries gives people the thrill of discovering new information, they're more likely to pay attention to places in nature they find mysterious than they are to natural places they already know and understand. Crop circles capture our attention well with their compelling works of art in nature's fields.

Public mysteries can divide people in intensely emotional ways. In our current divisive and mean-spirited culture, wonder is something we can all share that transcends our differences and helps us negotiate them. Despite our wildly different opinions on controversial mysteries, we can be inspired to learn how to work together because we're pursuing something greater than ourselves.

## EXPLORE PERSONAL MYSTERIES

I hung up the phone in my kitchen after hearing my beloved Grandma had passed away and sank into a chair like the weight of grief was pushing me down. Then I asked God to send Grandma my love and to send me a sign that she was in heaven. Immediately, a whirlwind blew on the deck outside, knocking potted plants over and making a loud whooshing sound. I rushed over to the sliding glass door and noticed the powerful wind was only present on my deck. Both of my next-door neighbors' decks—just a few feet away since we all lived in townhouses then—were still and quiet. Yet the wind swirled around my small deck, sending pieces of Honor's chalk flying around in the air. The sliding glass door shook from the wind's awesome power.

Then the wind defied the laws of physics as it moved inside my kitchen, even though I hadn't opened the door. The wind blew around where I stood, sending my hair flying and encasing me in a feeling of joy so intense I knew Grandma was in heaven. After a few euphoric moments, the wind shot back out the door and stopped. Everything outside was still again.

"He makes winds his messengers." (Psalm 104:4) came to mind as I pondered the mystery of the wondrous sign God had sent in response to my prayer. I didn't understand *how* the miraculous wind happened, but I did know *who* sent it, and I loved him even more for giving me that experience.

God sometimes sends mysterious signs and wonders into our personal lives to encourage us and strengthen our faith. We don't need to worry about figuring out exactly what they mean. We're free to receive those experiences as the gifts they are—if we let them motivate us to seek God more.

The purpose of God-given signs and wonders is always to inspire us to draw closer to him. God wants more from us than simply enjoying a thrill and moving on when he sends us a wonderful mystery. He wants us to believe in his power in deeper ways. Jesus miraculously healed a royal official's son who had been on verge of death when his father begged Jesus to intervene. The father didn't argue with Jesus about why his son was dying or doubt the mystery that healing was still possible. Even though Jesus chose to grant the father's request, he made an interesting comment: "Unless you people see signs and wonders," Jesus told him, "you will never believe" (John 4:48).

God seems to prefer that people believe in his power without needing signs and wonders to do so. But God is willing to send miracles into our lives when they serve the purpose of strengthening our faith. The father whose son Jesus healed showed faith in action when approaching God for a miracle. "'Go,' Jesus replied, 'your son will live.' The man took Jesus at his word and departed" (John 4:50). The rest of the story reveals that was the exact moment when the dying son was healed.

When we respond to mysteries by approaching God with faith—rather than trying to analyze, understand, or doubt what God chooses to do—we welcome potential miracles into our lives.

## INVESTIGATE WISELY

Mysteries both attract and repel us. We can be intrigued by what we don't understand and want to learn more. We can also be scared or threatened by the unknown. Too often, we find it easier to ignore mysteries rather than risk the mess of having them challenge our worldview. Mysteries can lead us to awe, if we don't let fear close our minds to learning from them. They call us to step out of our comfort zones and dance with our doubts and faith toward what may be something wonderful.

The way we respond to mysteries shows us where we're placing our faith. If our faith doesn't go beyond ourselves, we'll dismiss mysteries that are greater than our personal comfort zones—and in the process, we can miss many truly wondrous experiences. If we place our faith in mysterious signs and wonders themselves, we can be deceived by those mysteries, since we can be deceived by signs and wonders that come from negative sources, such as fallen angels (2 Thessalonians 2:9) and unfaithful people (Matthew 24:24). We can be greatly blessed if we place our faith in the giver—God—rather than the gift of mysteries and pay attention to what mysteries can tell us about him. The Bible often mentions holy signs and wonders that genuinely reflect God at work. Of course, the miracles of Jesus show that happening, but extraordinary signs and wonders also happened through the ordinary people who followed him. "Everyone was filled with awe at the many wonders and signs performed by the apostles" Acts 2:43 reveals.

Therefore, we must keep our minds open when we encounter mysteries and ask the Holy Spirit to give us the discernment we need to respond in wisely. We shouldn't be afraid, but neither should we be naïve.

In 1 John 4:1–3, the Bible explains a security system we can use when encountering mysterious signs and wonders: "Dear friends, do not believe every spirit, but test the spirits to see whether they are from God, because many false prophets have gone out into the world. This is how you can recognize the Spirit of God: Every spirit that acknowledges that Jesus Christ has come in the flesh is from God, but every spirit that does not acknowledge Jesus is not from God."

Think about this. We wouldn't leave the front door of our homes unlocked so anyone could walk in anytime, regardless of whether we knew and trusted them. That would be foolish. Our souls, which live forever, are even more valuable than our homes. So, it's vital to secure our souls spiritually as we would secure our home physically. We should check in with God about every mysterious wonder we encounter.

The mysteries from God are pure gifts. God isn't a magician or a cosmic vending machine who dispenses miracles on demand. He's a father who wants to build meaningful relationships with his children for good purposes, which can only happen when we decide to trust him rather than our own desires.

We can experience true wonder when we respond to the mysteries we encounter by seeking God's wisdom to help us learn from them. "There is a God in heaven who reveals mysteries," the Bible declares in Daniel 2:28. Mysteries themselves don't have any magical powers to unleash miracles for us. Instead, *the faith we express in response to mysteries* sends the wonder of miracles our way. God rewards the faith we show by moving closer to us, and the natural result of God coming closer to us is that we experience miracles. Miracles are simply messages from God. The closer our relationships with God become, the more we can perceive them. Miracles seem extraordinary to us when they're mysterious, but for God, they're simply business as usual. Genuine and positive mysteries help us notice the messages God is constantly communicating.

Mysteries can lead us to feel awe for God, who is beyond all limits and the source of all wonder. We invite God to turn mysteries into miracles in our lives when we dare to investigate mysteries with faith in God.

## QUESTIONS TO PONDER FOR WONDER

1. Which public mysteries inspire you and which disturb you? Why?
2. How can you move out of your comfort zone to try to learn from a personal mysterious experience?
3. What attitudes and actions are currently holding you back from living with an open mind and heart?
4. How can you practice discernment to protect yourself from deception and pursue wisdom from mysteries?
5. How can you remove some of the unnecessary limits you've placed on expressing your curiosity when encountering something you don't know, understand, or think is possible?

# Chapter 11

## Live with Purpose

"The … fat … cat … sat … on … the … mat." Justin sounded out the words carefully and then looked at Honor and me for approval.

I dropped the book on the floor in my excitement. My then-three-year-old had just read his first sentence.

"That's right, Justin," Honor declared, leaning over to give her brother a high-five.

A radiant smile spread across Justin's face. Then he picked up the book, flipped to the page with a drawing of an obese orange cat, and shouted out the sentence in victory.

That wondrous learning breakthrough happened because I focused on my purpose. Night after night at the dinner table, I read books to Justin, patiently pointing to each word, and then sounding out the letters for him. I had done so for Honor when she was the same age, and she had experienced a similar breakthrough. Plus, plenty of ordinary wonderful moments happened every night from simply exploring stories with my children, learning and laughing together. What kept me in a chair reading preschool books for hours—rather than other ways I could have used my evenings, like watching television— was remembering that using my time purposefully would lead to awe. I opened doors for wonder to walk through by doing my best with the role God had given me as a mom and putting into action the talents he gave me for communication and teaching.

Living with purpose helps us experience awe. Ephesians 2:10 reveals God has created us on purpose, as masterpieces, with good works planned for each of us to do in our earthly lifetimes. Part of our purpose is to discover those good works and pursue them faithfully. Our purpose integrates God's unique plan for our lives into everything we do. But God's purpose for us goes beyond *what we do* to *who we are*. Purpose is ultimately about the kind of people God wants us to become. Jesus described exactly what kind of people God is looking for after a man asked him about the greatest spiritual commandment. "Jesus replied: 'Love the Lord your God with all your heart and with all your soul and with all your mind.' This is the first and greatest commandment. And the second is like it: 'Love your neighbor as yourself.' All the Law and the Prophets hang on these two commandments" (Matthew 22:37–40).

Pursuing our purpose shouldn't be a complicated or confusing process. God made the procedure simple. Our purpose is simply to love. As we do our best to give and receive love—to God, ourselves, and others—we will experience the wonder of fulfilling our purpose day by day.

Experiencing awe can also help us focus on our purpose. Research shows feeling awe can strengthen our critical thinking abilities by alerting us to the gaps in our knowledge.[1] When we're able to think more critically about our lives, we can pursue more learning and discern God's purpose for us more clearly.

The more we base our decisions on God's love and wisdom flowing through our lives, the more we fulfill our purpose. That involves seeking inspiration from the Holy

Spirit day by day. Often, God will reveal only enough for us to take the next step he wants us to take rather than showing us a long-range plan. That's because God challenges us to trust him more each day. God would rather walk beside us personally on our journey than simply hand us a map to use by ourselves. The process of discovering and living out our purpose isn't complicated but happens naturally as we connect with God in a trusting relationship.

## CHOOSE THE BEST IDENTITY

I paced a hallway inside the Smithsonian Institution's National Museum of American History, trying to release the pent-up energy that made me feel like a balloon about to burst. I was going to meet my favorite classic movie star, Ginger Rogers, again. Talking with her the previous night at an American Film Institute event, I'd discovered the woman I had idolized for her glamorous elegance onscreen was simply another flesh-and-blood person. She was friendly—not aloof—so friendly, in fact, that she invited me to the museum today to see her donate a gown from the movie *Top Hat*, in which she danced with Fred Astaire. My watch revealed her public remarks were scheduled soon. I needed to return to my seat in the auditorium.

As I walked in front of an elevator, the doors opened, and suddenly Ginger and I were face to face. She looked just as surprised as I was, taking a step back for a moment and studying me carefully. "Oh, it's you, Whitney," she said once she recognized me. Her bright blonde hair and sky-blue blazer and skirt contrasted with the drab walls around us. It seemed as if she had stepped straight out of a movie into real life.

"It's you too, Ms. Rogers," I replied, feeling my face flush with embarrassment after those goofy words spilled out of my mouth.

"Yes, it is," she laughed. "I'm sneaking into the auditorium through the back way."

"Why?"

"I just want a break from the cameras after the press conference earlier today." She sighed, paused, and looked me in the eyes as if she was searching for something.

As a thirteen-year-old girl, I wasn't sure what I could offer her except respect and attentive listening. That's what had seemed to inspire her to talk to me candidly last night after we first met. I simply nodded with a smile.

"It's not always fun being famous," she said in a soft voice. "I know I have to be a 'movie star' every single time I go out in public. I'm grateful that people still appreciate my work. It's a blessing, but sometimes I just want to be myself."

"Um, why don't … What do you mean?" I stammered, surprised this star who had been in front of cameras for many years struggled with her fame. "Don't you enjoy being photographed?"

"Oh, my—not all the time." Ginger replied. "It can be stressful and sometimes even scary if people are pushing cameras in my face and shouting at me to sign autographs for them."

"Wow. That would be a challenge. I guess I don't know what it's like to go through that."

Ginger paused for a long moment and seemed to be reflecting on something. "I don't mind playing this movie star role when I have to," she finally said. "But my real identity is something better."

"Your real identity?"

She nodded as a radiant smile spread across her face. "I'm a child of God. That's my real identity. Same as you."

Ginger's words shattered my illusions. I'd idolized her for her glamorous image, yet she pointed me toward the only one truly worthy of worshiping—God. Before I could think of how to reply, she spoke again. "Well, I've got to go. The team is probably wondering where I am. See you in the auditorium."

"Thanks. See you there."

A few minutes later, I joined my dad and sister in the auditorium to watch Ginger introduce a screening of *Top Hat*. I waved to her after she spoke, and she waved back. Then, when her image appeared on the gigantic screen, I realized what I saw was only an image. The real Ginger—and the real me—had much greater identities than what could show up on a screen.

Each of us has an identity that transcends whatever roles we play or how other people perceive us. Every one of us has an identity that is nothing less than this—God's beloved child, made in his image, for a wonderful purpose. Seeing ourselves as God sees us can lead to wonder because the process enlarges our perspective. A research study found people who felt wonder from awe-inspiring experiences report their perspectives became greater as a result. From the enlarged perspective wonder gave them, they said they felt more compassion, gratitude, love, and optimism, and connectedness.[2]

When we're connected to Jesus in a relationship, we're "a chosen people" who "may declare the praises of him who called you out of darkness into his wonderful light." (1

Peter 2:9). The journey we take with God out of darkness into light helps us see every situation from a greater perspective, which reveals God's goodness at work. By centering ourselves in the truth of who we are from God's perspective, we position ourselves to perceive wonder and share it with others.

## TAKE ACTION WHEN GOD CALLS

Holding newborn Honor as she slept peacefully against my chest, I shuddered to think how close she had come to dying before she had a chance to be born. I kissed her peach fuzz hair and snuggled close to her for a few quiet moments. Then the loud ring of our telephone jolted my mind back to the day my friend Gigi called early one morning before Honor's birth.

"You were on my mind last night when I woke up, and I felt an urge to pray for you," Gigi had told me. "Don't be afraid, but I really think you need to visit your doctor for a sonogram today. While I prayed, I had a strong sense your doctor needs to see your baby. Please try to get a sonogram done today if you can."

Gigi's words hit me like splash of cold water in my face. Yet I knew her to be a trustworthy friend and a reasonable person. "I, I, um …" I stammered, trying not to become too upset at what might be wrong with my unborn daughter, who was nearly two weeks late arriving already.

"Don't worry, Whitney. Just call and let the doctor's office know you're coming in today to check on the baby," Gigi told me in a kind but firm voice.

Soon after hanging up, I drove straight to my obstetrician's office and waited for her in person until she was done with an appointment. Calmly, I asked her for an emergency sonogram, explaining the conversation I'd had with Gigi. The doctor rolled her eyes like she thought I was crazy. She told me she knew of no medical reason that would justify the sonogram, she was too busy today, and my insurance wouldn't cover it since she didn't recommend it. "Just go home," she said. But I insisted on the sonogram before leaving the office, so the doctor finally relented.

The doctor's eyes widened with alarm as she watched the image on the sonogram screen. "The baby is so overdue the placenta is breaking down," she blurted out. "I must have miscalculated your due date. If we don't act soon, your baby could be stillborn. Go to the hospital right away, so we can induce labor."

I did as she instructed and was deeply grateful to both God and Gigi when Honor was born healthy soon afterward.

A vital part of living with purpose is being willing to act whenever we sense God calling us to do something. Because God often works through people, we could become part of a miracle simply by saying "yes" when the Holy Spirit nudges us to proceed. Sometimes, those nudges feel like being led to the top a cliff and encouraged to jump off. God constantly challenges us to grow our faith, and we may not understand why he leads us to move forward or what will happen after we do. But remember—our purpose is all about love. The more we choose to respond in love when God calls us, the less fear we'll experience. First John 4:18 promises: "There is no fear in love. But perfect love drives out fear." Wonder rushes into our lives when we drive fear out. Research has found experiencing awe in the face of uncertainty increases belief in the supernatural (such as God's guidance), as well as the ability to perceive that events aren't random, but instead happen because of a greater purpose.[3]

## USE YOUR TALENTS

Looking inside NASA's historic Apollo Mission Control Center, Honor and I monitored the same complex data that NASA employees did on the day when humans first landed on the moon—July 20, 1969. Lines stretched across graphs, numbers marched across screens, and coded buttons flashed on and off in this reenactment of how the mission enfolded. Recordings of voice communication between the astronauts in space and mission control workers at the Johnson Space Center in Texas from that day played in sync with the data display. We watched charts map the lunar module's descent and finally celebrated its landing. That recreated moment, which happened before either of us was born, felt as wondrous as if we had experienced it ourselves.

One woman's talents had been vital to the success of the moon landing, which inspired worldwide wonder that day. Katherine Johnson, a brilliant mathematician, performed the critical calculations that kept the Lunar Module in sync with the orbiting Command and Service Module. She also made significant contributions to NASA's rocket launches, Space Shuttle program, and Earth Resources Satellite. Katherine saw her talents as gifts from God. Her confidence that God had given her those talents for good purposes motivated her to develop and use them. Even though Katherine faced discrimination as a Black woman from a poor family, she courageously persisted in seeking opportunities to learn more and contribute more.

"I counted everything," she recalled of her childhood. "I counted the steps to the road, the steps to the church, the number of dishes and silverware I washed … anything that could be counted, I did." Katherine's determination to use her math talents eventually led to her helping desegregate West Virginia University's graduate school, becoming a teacher, and then working for NASA. Beyond her renowned contributions to space exploration, Katherine faithfully used her math talents in other ways, such as serving as the finance committee chairperson for her church and providing free math tutoring for students.

Katherine often encouraged others to discover their own God-given talents by pursuing their natural interests. She urged people to "Like what you do, and then you will do your best."

As Honor and I walked out of the historic mission control, I said a silent prayer asking God to keep encouraging Honor to use her talents. Honor, a college student studying engineering and physics, is gifted in math just as Katherine was. I'm proud of my daughter and many other people I know who are seeking to use the talents God gave them for good purposes. We all have important contributions to make to this world—and we do so best by putting our talents into action.

Experiencing wonder can inspire us to use our talents more. When people feel awe, they can become motivated to learn more and create more—tapping into their personal talents in the process, research shows.[4]

In 1 Peter 4:10, the apostle Peter encouraged all believers to use the abilities God gave them to serve others for the common good. We are connected to each other in a network where God's love flows between us as we use our talents. The more we each contribute, the more wonder we can all experience as a result.

## QUESTIONS TO PONDER FOR WONDER

1. What has your journey to discovering your purpose been like so far? How does focusing on love day by day help you?

2. What is one loving choice you can make today that will help you live with greater purpose?

3. How do you feel about your identity as a person right now? What will help you identify yourself as God's beloved child, regardless of what other roles you play or how others see you?

4. When did you recently say or do something in response to God's leading? How did that result in wonder happening?

5. What are some of your God-given talents? How can you use them in ways that contribute more wonder to our world?

# Chapter 12

## Worship with Wonder

Water flowed with ferocious speed over Niagara Falls as our tour boat approached. I gripped the boat's railings with both hands and breathed deeply to try to stay calm as I came face to face with the waterfall's raw power. Each of my senses became overwhelmed with wonder as about six million cubic feet of water per minute cascaded down. A wall of white, blue, and green flooded my entire field of vision. The clean scent of water refreshed me. A thundering sound reverberated through my body. Cold sprays of water drenched my face and rain poncho. I could even taste the purity of the mist. Feelings of elation and fear flowed through my mind as the water flowed over the Niagara Gorge. Even as I enjoyed its awesome beauty, I knew Niagara Falls could engulf me completely if I came too close. Overwhelmed by the power of the water, I reached my hands out closer to the massive spray and praised God for what his design had made possible.

Worship is a natural response when we wake up to the wonder around us. Awe inspires our souls to celebrate the ultimate source of wonder—God. The connection between wonder and worship works the other way around, as well. Research shows the more people identify themselves as spiritual (including putting their spirituality in action through worship), the more likely they are to feel awe.[1] People who regularly attend worship services are also more likely than others to manage stress well and experience strong mental and physical health (all of which can help them discover more wonder), according to research.[2] Research even shows participating regularly in a worship community can help people live longer than those who don't do so—possibly because they're connected to something greater than themselves.[3]

Worship is a lifestyle we can enjoy anytime and anywhere. Approaching worship as a lifestyle will bring us into contact with wonder on a regular basis, as our worship connects us with God, the ultimate source of wonder.

## FOCUS ON GOD'S PRESENCE

As I wrote an article, a ping sound notified me of an email from the media company where I worked. Stressful phrases such as "urgent request," "significant change," and "tight deadline" jumped off the screen at me. My company had decided to change its content policies to work with new search engine algorithms. Executives were asking us editors to update as many articles as we could on our websites within a short time. My site featured hundreds of articles, so I faced a daunting task. The stress of the surprise request on top my many current assignments made my heartbeat race. Still, I was up to the challenge.

Hunkering down over my computer keyboard, I furiously scanned through articles and made notes on how I could update them. But my pounding heartbeat kept signaling I needed to take a break. I stopped to refresh my glass of water and was about to return to work when I realized I needed more refreshment than a drink. I needed to feel awe from a fresh encounter with God.

Worship was calling to my soul. I answered by driving to a local church, which welcomed people to pray in its sanctuary anytime. In that place dedicated to God, I thanked him for the opportunity to help people worldwide through my work and asked for the strength to keep serving well. "'Be still, and know that I am God'" (Psalm 46:10) came to mind. The stillness seemed to be embracing me with a sense of peace, which left no room for stress to linger. How could I worry about my schedule in the presence of the One who invented time itself? All would be well, I knew. I didn't know *how* I'd get everything done, but I knew *Who* would help me do so.

Work had been an idol for me in the past, and worship was the antidote to falling into idolatry again. We all must guard ourselves against idols that distract us from the only one worthy of worship—God. Every human being worships someone or something. We can choose to devote ourselves primarily to God by investing most of our time and energy into a relationship with him. If we neglect to do that, some type of idol will consume the attention that we should be devoting to God. Possible idols include work, power, money, possessions, sex, fitness, leisure, success, appearance, drugs, relationships, education, titles, sports teams, and even religious activities. We must be willing to give God first place in our lives to stay centered and encounter wonder regularly.

Besides focusing our worship on God, we also need to approach him with pure motives. Jesus confronted religious leaders called the Pharisees about their approach to worship, calling them "hypocrites" because "they honor me with their lips, but their hearts are far from me. They worship me in vain; their teachings are merely human rules'" (Matthew 15:7-9). Although the Pharisees publicly declared their love for God, love didn't motivate their worship. Jesus, who could see into their minds and hearts, said that, in truth, they were worshiping to gain public favor for themselves instead of to express real love for God. God is interested in relationships, not religious duties motivated by obligation, guilt, pride, or manipulation. Our motives are pure when we can honestly say we're choosing to worship to express our love for God and thank God for loving us.

The goal of worship is to experience the presence of God. Acts chapter 17 describes God's awe-inspiring generosity toward humankind and then proclaims God intends for people to discover his presence with them. "God did this so that they would seek him and perhaps reach out for him and find him, though he is not far from any one of us. 'For in him we live and move and have our being.' As some of your own poets have said, 'We are his offspring.'" (Acts 17:27-28). Worship helps us become aware of God's constant presence among us. When we expect God to show up as we gather to worship him together, our minds and hearts are ready to perceive the wonder of his presence with us.

## WORSHIP IN SPIRIT AND TRUTH

Our congregation worshiped in church as a thunderstorm raged outside. We sang along with the worship team to the pulsating beats of a song as colorful beams of light danced above us. Then, a few seconds after a loud thunderclap, the band fell silent and darkness filled our sanctuary as our church lost electrical power. "Let's wait a while to see if the power will come back on," our pastor suggested, projecting his voice as much as he could without a microphone. As we waited, the storm's sounds spoke to us of nature's awesome energy. Wind whooshed, thunder rumbled and cracked, and rain deluged the church's roof in a torrential downpour.

Conversations about the storm began throughout the sanctuary. Russ and I turned to a couple sitting next to us to chat with them. "When I was growing up, my parents told me the sound of thunder was God bowling in heaven," said Mirabel, who was there with her husband David. "Really? My mom told me that, too," I said as we all laughed.

"Storms can generate a lot of electrical energy," Russ said. "I read that scientists used a cosmic ray detector to measure the energy of one thunderstorm at more than one billion volts."

"Wow," David, Mirabel, and I exclaimed together, united by our sense of awe.

"I love seeing photos of lightning," said Mirabel. "You can see the power of the electrical energy so vividly in them."

"They look like veins of light reaching out of the sky," I said.

While the storm continued its rampage outside, David suggested we pray together for the safety of everyone in the church building. "God answered a similar prayer for us and our children during another severe thunderstorm," he told us. "We had a dying tree outside our daughter's bedroom window. We'd gotten an estimate for the cost of removing it and were saving up to get the removal done when the storm happened. All we could do then was pray. We sat in our living room together with flashlights after the power went out, asking God to send angels to protect us and our neighbors from harm. As a precaution, we slept downstairs in sleeping bags rather than go back up to the bedrooms, but we felt at peace. Later that night, the tree did fall, but not on our house or on our neighbors' house next door. Even though it was leaning toward our house, the tree fell in a way that didn't make sense physically, in the narrow space between the two houses, like it had been carefully laid down in the grass there."

After reveling in the wonder of David's story, we held hands and prayed together, asking God to protect our congregation from harm. We had only just met each other. Still, as I felt Mirabel's pulse while we held hands, I knew we were connected in a spiritual family. Through worship, we connected as brothers and sisters communicating with our heavenly father.

The church's electrical power remained off, so everyone went home without more music or even a sermon that Sunday. Yet we had still worshiped, as awe brought us closer to God and each other.

Worship transcends the details of any one service. So what if the music or liturgy isn't what we're used to, or what we prefer? When we're truly aware of God's presence with us, none of that matters. The point of worship isn't entertainment. This is our time to encounter God and respond to his love together.

Every worship experience can wake us up to wonder more by showing us additional ways to worship God with our diverse family of spiritual brothers and sisters. The peaceful quiet of a Quaker service in a simple meeting house, the beauty of the icons at an ornate Orthodox church, the invigorating altar call at a Baptist church—all have the power to draw us closer to God and each other.

Expanding the way we worship is vital to keep it from degenerating into a boring routine—or worse, an obligatory chore. Worship is meant to lead us to wonder by centering our hearts and minds on the source of wonder—

God. Jesus has revealed the essence of what God is looking for in worship: "The true worshipers will worship the Father in spirit and truth" (John 4:23). Worshiping like that involves engaging our emotions in loving communication with God's Spirit while focusing our thoughts on the truth about who God is.

## EXPRESS GRATITUDE

At a hospital with a chaplain I was shadowing for a newspaper article, we stepped inside the room of a cancer patient named Kaylie, who looked about eight years old. She smiled underneath her oxygen mask as the chaplain prayed for her. Afterward, Kaylie commented, "Thanks. I'm glad to still be here to see you today."

"I'm grateful to see you again, too, Kaylie," the chaplain replied. "Every day is a gift."

"Yeah—and really, every breath we take is a gift," she replied in a quiet voice under the constant hum of the oxygen.

I thought of a statistic I'd read. Every person inhales and exhales about twenty thousand times or more, every day. Even something as simple as breathing is a profound gift from God.

God is constantly pouring blessings into our lives, even during challenging circumstances. Choosing to be grateful for those blessings opens doors that lead to wonder, by giving us a greater perspective on our circumstances. A research study of people dealing with the constant stress of chronic illness found those whose spirituality or religion motivated them to be grateful for their blessings experienced awe as a result—despite the stress of dealing with disease. But those who didn't express faith missed out on awe.[4]

Multiple research studies show people who regularly choose an attitude of gratitude experience a myriad of benefits. These include significantly higher levels of positive emotions (including joy, which leads to awe). Also, they are more alert (and therefore more able to notice wonder) than those who don't give thanks regularly.[5] The benefits of gratitude are so numerous they impact every aspect of our lives. Each of those benefits is correlated with happiness and joy, which point us in the direction of wonder.[6]

The root of the word "gratitude" is the Latin word *gratus*, which is also the root of the word "grace." When we choose to be grateful, we become full of grace. In a state of gratitude, we can perceive the wonder of God's love and wisdom around us. We can also participate in that wonder by allowing God's Spirit to work through us. How often do we take God's simple yet profound gifts for granted, instead of fully appreciating them? Whenever we intentionally thank God for the gifts he constantly pours into our lives, we can experience awe.

What are you especially grateful for right now? Do you have family and friends who love you? Are you enjoying good health? Does your job give you opportunities to use your talents? When you pray, mention specific blessings, and express your gratitude to God bringing those blessings into your life. You could use prayer beads to count your blessings as you pray.

Create some rituals to celebrate evidence of God's work in your life day by day. Each morning after you wake up or each evening at bedtime, you could write a list of several blessings you're thankful for in a gratitude journal. At dinner, you could talk with your family about how you all encountered God during work or school and why you're grateful for that. At church, you could spend some time reflecting on the ultimate sacrifice Jesus made on the cross before taking communion, so gratitude will be fresh on your mind when you celebrate communion (also called the Eucharist, which means "give thanks" in Greek).

Learning to be content—no matter what's happening in your life—helps you learn to be grateful in any situation because you're acknowledging that God will accomplish good purposes even through the bad circumstances in your life. Research has found choosing to be grateful even in bad circumstances decreases negative emotional responses to those circumstances.[7] The apostle Paul wrote: "I have learned to be content whatever the circumstances" (Philippians 4:11). Humble yourself to absorb the reality that everything you have is because of God's generosity. While God loves you completely, he owes you nothing. Get rid of an entitlement attitude and simply receive the blessings he chooses to send you as the pure gifts they are. Choose to appreciate whatever you have—either a lot or a little—at any given time.

Expressing gratitude to God is a form of worship that enlarges our perspective, which helps us perceive the wonder around us in any situation.

## GIVE GOD PRAISE

Glancing at the clock in my hospital room, I thought of our church's Christmas Eve service starting across town. This would be the first time since I'd come to faith years ago that I missed church on Christmas. A twinge of regret moved through me, even though I knew God wouldn't be angry about my absence. I had a great excuse—only yesterday, I'd given birth to our son, Justin. I still longed to be at church, praising God in a festive Christmas Eve atmosphere of twinkling lights, fragrant evergreens, and dramatic music. I wanted to celebrate. At the same time, a sense of dread crept up on me like a thief trying to steal my joy. Justin's routine newborn baby lab tests indicated the possibility of a serious health problem. Doctors expressed concern and ordered more testing right away.

Justin slept peacefully while mixed emotions churned through me. Reaching for one of his tiny feet, I traced the bumpy place on his sole where blood had been drawn for the lab tests. Then Justin opened his eyes, and I gazed into them. The light of Justin's soul shone out of his eyes as we looked at each other with love. In the wonder of that moment, I was no longer concerned about being stuck in an austere hospital room on Christmas Eve, nor worried about facing the future with uncertainty about Justin's health. Awe showed me God was right there.

"Thank you, God," I said in spontaneous praise. "Justin is the best Christmas present I've ever gotten." When all the Christmas worship traditions were stripped away, what mattered most about Christmas—God's presence—remained. I thought of Jesus in the manger as I looked at my son in his bassinet. Justin was simply an ordinary human baby, but I was still looking at a miracle.

The next day, on Christmas morning, the additional lab test results revealed Justin was healthy. That was yet another gift for which I was grateful, but I was glad I hadn't waited for my uncertainty to be resolved before choosing to praise God.

God is worthy of praise in any circumstances—the good, the bad, and the in-between situations—because he is always there for us, offering love and wisdom. Praising God is like opening a door to our lives and welcoming God inside. Psalm 22:3 declares God inhabits (or is enthroned on) the praises of his people. When we worship through praise, God meets with us and we feel the awe of his presence among us. Praise is like opening a door for God to walk through. Praise welcomes the wonder that God wants to send into our lives.

## WORSHIP TOGETHER IN COMMUNITY

My car suddenly lost power, slowing abruptly in the middle of traffic. I gripped the steering wheel and swung hard to the right. As my heartbeat sped up in a panic, I maneuvered my car to the shoulder of the road and prayed for help. A tapping sound drew my attention immediately afterward to a man in a car mechanic's uniform. He was knocking on my window. As our eyes met, he smiled and gestured toward a tow truck nearby. I rolled down the window. "Hi, I'm Richard," he said. "There's a gas station just across the street. I won't charge you to tow the car that short distance. Then we can figure out how to fix your car."

Cautiously, I got out. "Thanks," I told him. "I'm surprised you got here so quickly. My car only just now broke down."

"I know. I saw it happen," he replied.

After the brief journey to the station, Richard disappeared into the service bay, and I paced around the parking lot for a while. My car was a cheap old clunker. That was all I could afford as a college student. *How expensive is this repair going to be?*

Then Richard emerged from the service bay. "It was your alternator," he announced in a soothing voice. "Don't worry—the replacement is inexpensive."

I relaxed when I saw the affordable price. "That's great. I sure don't want to be without my car this week with everything I'm planning to do."

"Yes, all your classes—and the campus ministry's worship service, too, right?"

"Um, yeah," I said, startled since I didn't recall mentioning my schedule details to Richard. "I'm a student at George Mason University."

He nodded as if he already knew.

"I don't think I mentioned that," I said quizzically.

"I hope you go to the worship service," Richard replied, breezing past my puzzlement. "Yes, it can be intimidating to walk into a group event when you don't know anyone yet. Ask for Susan. She's a caring person who's great at welcoming people."

"Well, I don't know. I'm shy." I was intrigued by the Bible now that I was reading it thoroughly for the first time and trying to apply the words to my life. I was truly seeking God, but the thought of joining a worship service full of strangers scared me. I reasoned I could read the Bible and pray by myself. I'd picked up a flyer about the campus service but had recently decided not to attend.

"You know, it's important to seek God in community," Richard continued, as if he could read my mind. "God is pleased you're reading scripture now, but you'll learn much more if you worship in the company of others. Just go to the service this week. You'll make some good friends there."

"What? How? Do you know the people in the campus ministry?"

He nodded. "I know all of them."

"Were you a member? Did you go to Mason?"

Richard laughed heartily. "No, I've never shown up there before, but this isn't about me. It's about God." He paused and looked at me intently, like he could see into my soul. "Have courage. Promise me that you'll go to the worship service just to give it a try."

"Um, well, I guess," I managed as I gazed back at him.

"You promise?" His smile was so disarming that all my fears faded away.

"Sure," I finally said.

"Great," he replied as joy radiated across his round face. He reached into his pocket and handed me my car key, the amazingly low repair bill, and a business card. "You can check out with the cashier, and then you're all set to go. I've got to get back. Enjoy the campus service."

I thanked him and glanced down at the business card while he walked away. Instead of the gas station's information, I found only two sentences printed on it: "You may not remember me. But always remember the One who sent me."

Curious, I asked the cashier about Richard, and she said the station didn't have any employees with that name. I walked around trying to find him, to no avail. When I asked the station's manager and other employees on duty about Richard, they had no knowledge of a mechanic by that name. All they knew was a man had towed my car to the station and told them to replace the alternator with a new one he'd taken out of his tow truck.

I believe I encountered the wonder of an angel appearing in human form that day.

My old car worked well for years after that mysterious breakdown. Much more importantly, my faith was working well—because I had found a caring worship community.

Community is a vital part of worship, because God has designed us all to be connected to him and each other in bonds of love. The Bible mentions worship in heaven includes "a great multitude that no one could count, from every nation, tribe, people and language" (Revelation 7:9). Whenever we worship in community here on earth, we're preparing our souls to worship one day with the great multitude of believers standing before God's heavenly throne.

Research shows contemplative spiritual practices such as worship "strengthen a specific neurological circuit that generates peacefulness, social awareness, and compassion for others."[8] A study also suggests experiencing awe can reduce polarization and increase a sense of community between people by helping them be more humble and feel more connected to each other.[9]

Moments of wonder during worship reveal how worship connects us with God and each other. Once, I visited the Portiuncula, a chapel where many people have gathered to pray over the centuries since Saint Francis of Assisi often prayed there. I sat among the diverse people praying in the pews and focused my attention on seeking God in that present moment. Soon, I felt a powerful sensation like someone pouring warm honey all over me. A mental feeling of pure bliss accompanied the physical feeling, and a thought filled my mind. *God loves me completely and unconditionally, and there is nothing I can do to either earn or lose his love.* While I enjoyed feeling God's love, I also realized the experience wasn't for me alone. I sensed God connecting all the people in prayer around me to him—and to each other—by the power of love, which energetically embraced us. Time stood still for me as I savored the wonder of that experience. I only realized after I finally left and checked the time on my phone that I'd been sitting there for almost an hour feeling the Holy Spirit's embrace. After I left the chapel, the warm honey feeling melted away, and I emerged awed and humbled by having felt the spiritual energy of God's love at work.

## QUESTIONS TO PONDER FOR WONDER

1. How much time and energy are you currently devoting to your relationship with God? What idols may be taking your attention away from God, and how can you control them so they stop controlling you?

2. How could you expand the way you worship? What changes could you make to your worship routine? When could you visit a church with a different worship style from your home church to connect with God in fresh ways?

3. What blessings are you especially grateful for right now and why?

4. When were you able to praise God during challenging circumstances? How did your focus on praise help you perceive more of God's work in that situation?

5. Who could you build closer relationships with by pursuing wonder together regularly?

# Conclusion

One summer night in the Berkshires of Massachusetts, I ventured outside my lodge to enjoy a walk among gigantic evergreen trees. Balsam fir, spruce, and pine trees stretched their majestic needled branches out as if embracing the pure forest air. As they towered over me, their dark silhouettes in the moonlight seemed to reach up to the moon itself. Overcome by awe, I began an impromptu prayer walk among the trees to thank God and enjoy what he had created. The sky glittered with stars above the trees. I walked into a field to get a closer look at them and thank God for the awesome scenery. Then a shooting star streaked right in front of me. Its brilliant light reminded me that wonder follows wonder.

Worship is the end of our journey toward wonder together. When we encounter wonder, we realize how awesome God is, and we naturally respond by worshiping.

Wonder never ends, but operates in a cycle. The more we let awe inspire us, the closer we can grow to God, and the more wonder we can enjoy as a result. Every moment of our lives is a fresh opportunity to experience awe. Along the way, however, we must remain committed to the practices that welcome wonder into our daily lives. We need to pray and meditate, manage stress well, overcome fear, pursue lifelong learning, use our senses, manage time well, enjoy nature, renew our minds, explore mysteries, live with purpose, and worship.

# Wake Up to Wonder

Now that we have woken up to wonder, let's remain awake. Let's look for the everyday miracles around us, savor feelings of awe at every opportunity, and enjoy the adventure.

# About the Author

Whitney Hopler writes the *Wake Up to Wonder* blog on her website, whitneyhopler.com. Whitney's writing has inspired many readers worldwide. Her articles have appeared in leading publications, such as *Angels on Earth*, *The Washington Post*, and Thrive Global.com. Whitney has authored several previous books, such as the young adult novel *Dream Factory* and the nonfiction book *A Creative Life: God's Design for You*. She has also contributed to successful compilation books published by *Guideposts* and *Chicken Soup for the Soul*. Whitney has served as a writer, editor, and website developer for top media organizations, including Crosswalk.com, The Salvation Army USA's national publications, and Dotdash.com (where she produced a popular channel on angels and miracles). Currently, she leads the communications work for the Center for the Advancement of Well-Being at George Mason University.

## Introduction

[1] "The Science of Awe." September 2018. Greater Good Science Center at UC Berkeley. https://ggsc.berkeley.edu/images/uploads/GGSC-JTF_White_Paper-Awe_FINAL.pdf

[2] Goodreads.com. "Albert Einstein > Quotes > Quotable Quote." Accessed April 17, 2020. https://www.goodreads.com/quotes/987-there-are-only-two-ways-to-live-your-life-one

## Chapter 1

[1] Zeki, Semir. *Inner Vision: An Exploration of Art and the Brain*. Oxford, England: Oxford University Press, 2000.

[2] Newberg, Andrew, Thomas Jefferson University and Hospital. "How Do Meditation and Prayer Change Our Brains?" Accessed September 6, 2019. http://www.andrewnewberg.com/research

[3] Luhrmann, T., Stanford University, Nusbaum, H. and Thisted, R., University of Chicago (2013). "'Lord, Teach Us to Pray': Prayer Practice Affects Cognitive Processing." *Journal of Cognition and Culture*, volume: 13, pages: 1-2, DOI: 10.1163/15685373-12342090

[4] Zeki, Semir. *Inner Vision: An Exploration of Art and the Brain*. Oxford, England: Oxford University Press. 2000.

Graham, J., University of Southern California, Valdesolo, P., Claremont McKenna College (2013). "Awe, Uncertainty, and Agency Detection." *Journal of Psychological Science* volume: 25, issue: 1, page(s): 170-178, DOI: 10.1177/0956797613501884

[5] Pryce, P. University of British Columbia (2019). "Forming 'Mediators and Instruments of Grace: The

Emerging Role of Monastics in Teaching Contemplative Ambiguity and Practice to the Laity." *Religions, volume: 10, Issue:* 7, page: 405, DOI: 10.3390/rel10070405

[6] Colzato, L., Szapora, A., Lippelt, D., and Hommel, B. Leiden University (2014). "Prior Meditation Practice Modulates Performance and Strategy Use in Convergent- and Divergent-Thinking Problems." *Mindfulness*, volume 8: issue 1, pages: 10-16.

## Chapter 2

[1] Stress in America survey, 2013. American Psychological Association

[2] Q1 2018 Nielson Total Audience Report

[3] "Public Health Implications of Excessive Use of the Internet and Other Communication and Gaming Platforms." September 2018. World Health Organization

[4] "Workaholism in America." 2017. Business Insurance Quotes

[5] "The 2019 Year in Review." December 2019. PornHub.com. Accessed February 22, 2020. https://www.pornhub.com/insights/2019-year-in-review.

[6] "More Americans Say Pornography is Morally Acceptable." June 2018. Gallup.

[7] "Global Status Report on Alcohol and Health." 2018. World Health Organization. and "Management of Substance Abuse: Facts and Figures." 2018. World Health Organization.

[8] Burgess, L. "Eight Benefits of Crying: Why It's Good to Shed a Few Tears." October 2017. MedicalNewsToday.com.

[9] Kao, F.C., Wang, S. & Chang, Y.J. 2015. *Brainwaves Analysis of Positive and Negative Emotions*. Da-Yeh University, Taiwan

[10] Law, E., Girgis, A., Sylvie, L., Levesque, J., & Pickett, H. 2016. "Telomeres and Stress: Promising Avenues for Research in Psycho-Oncology." *Asia-Pacific Journal of Oncology Nursing, 3*(2), 137-147.

[11] Bhasin M.K., Dusek JA, Chang B-H, Joseph MG, Denninger JW, Fricchione GL, et al. 2013. "Relaxation Response Induces Temporal Transcriptome Changes in Energy Metabolism, Insulin Secretion and Inflammatory Pathways." *PLoS ONE* 8(5): e62817. https://doi.org/10.1371/journal.pone.0062817.

[12] McTaggart, Lynne. *The Power of Eight: Harnessing the Miraculous Energies of a Small Group to Heal Others, Your Life, and the World.* New York: Atria Books, Simon & Schuster, Inc.. 2017.

[13] Hopler, W. "How Walking Can Set Your Mental Well-Being in the Right Direction." Thrive Global.com. Accessed September 6, 2019. https://thriveglobal.com/stories/how-walking-can-set-your-mental-well-being-in-the-right-direction/.

[14] Ariga, A. and Lleras, A. 2011. "Break and Rare Mental 'Breaks' Keep You Focused: Deactivation and Reactivation of Task Goals Preempt Vigilance Decrements." *Cognition.* 118:3. 439-43.

[15] Immordino-Yang, M., Christodoulou, J., Singh, V. 2012. "Rest is Not Idleness: Implications of the Brain's Default Mode for Human Development and Education". *Perspectives on Psychological Science.* 7:4.352-364.

## Chapter 3

[1] GodTube staff. *Great is Thy Faithfulness.* GodTube.com Accessed April 17, 2020. https://www.godtube.com/popular-hymns/great-is-thy-faithfulness/

[2] Rankin, K., Andrews, S., and Sweeny, K. (2019): "Awe-full Uncertainty: Easing Discomfort during Waiting Periods." The Journal of Positive Psychology, DOI:10.108 0/17439760.2019.1615106

## Chapter 4

[1] Horrigan, John. "Lifelong Learning and Technology." Pew Research Center, March 22, 2016. https://www. pewinternet.org/2016/03/22/lifelong-learning-and-technology/.

[2] Hadzigeorgiou, Yannis. "Fostering a Sense of Wonder in the Science Classroom." University of the Aegean. 2011.

[3] L'Ecuyer Catherine. "The Wonder Approach to Learning." *Frontiers in Human Neuroscience*. October 6, 2014. 8:764. doi: 10.3389/fnhum.2014.00764. eCollection 2014. PMID: 25339882

[4] Glaveanu, Vlad. "Creativity and Wonder." *Journal of Creative Behavior*, Volume 53, Issue 2, June 2019, https://doi.org/10.1002/jocb.225

[5] Rudd, Melanie, Vohs, Kathleen. "Inspired to Create: How Awe Enhances Openness to Learning and Desire for Experiential Creation." The Association for Consumer Research. 2015.

[6] Kashdan, Todd., Stiksma, Melissa, Disabato, David, McKnight, David, Bekier, John, Kaji, Joel, Lazarus, Rachel. "The Five-Dimensional Curiosity Scale Revised (5DCR)." George Mason University, Time, Inc., and Marketing and Research Resources, Inc. 2019.

[7] Billington, Josie. "Reading between the Lines: the Benefits of Reading for Pleasure." Quick Reads, University of Liverpool. 2015.

[8] Geisel, Theodor. 1978. *I Can Read with My Eyes Shut!* New York: Random House.

[9] Gray, Brianna and Rosch, Jake. *Talking in Class: Increasing the Quality and Quantity of Student-to-Student Dialogue in the Classroom.* London: ACS International Schools. 2018.

[10] Taylor, Mia. "New Research Findings Show Wonder of Travel is Being Lost." Travel Pulse.com, October 23, 2018. https://www.travelpulse.com/news/tour-operators/new-research-findings-show-wonder-of-travel-is-being-lost.html.

[11] Taylor, Mia. "New Research Findings Show Wonder of Travel is Being Lost." Travel Pulse.com, October 23, 2018. https://www.travelpulse.com/news/tour-operators/new-research-findings-show-wonder-of-travel-is-being-lost.html.

[12] Wei, Sherrie and Milman, Ady. "The Impact of Participation in Activities while on Vacation on Seniors' Psychological Well-Being: A Path Model Application." University of Queensland-Gatton, University of Central Florida. 2002.

[13] Goodreads. "Augustine of Hippo > Quotes > Quotable Quote." Goodreads.com. Accessed April 17, 2020. https://www.goodreads.com/quotes/6193-the-world-is-a-book-and-those-who-do-not.

[14] Harvard Health Publishing. "Learning While You Sleep: Dream or Reality?" Harvard Medical School, February 2012. https://www.health.harvard.edu/staying-healthy/learning-while-you-sleep-dream-or-reality.

[15] Tesla, Nikola. *My Inventions: The Autobiography of Nikola Tesla.* New York. Experimenter Publishing Company. 1919.

[16] Tesla, Nikola. "The Problem of Increasing Human Energy." *The Century Illustrated Monthly Magazine*, Volume 38; Volume 60.

[17] Tesla, Nikola. *My Inventions: The Autobiography of Nikola Tesla*. New York. Experimenter Publishing Company. 1919.

**Chapter 5**

[1] Zeki, Semir. *Inner Vision: An Exploration of Art and the Brain*. Oxford, England. Oxford University Press. 2000.

[2] Baker, Mitzi. "Music Moves Brain to Pay Attention, Stanford Study Finds." *Stanford Medicine*. Stanford University. Aug. 1, 2007. med.stanford.edu/news/all-news/2007/07/music-moves-brain-to-pay-attention-stanford-study-finds.html.

[3] Hopler, W. "Music and Well-Being: Using the Energy of Sound for Healing." Thrive Global.com. Nov. 8, 2018. https://thriveglobal.com/stories/music-and-well-being-using-the-energy-of-sound-for-healing/.

[4] Ibid.

[5] Quing, L. (2010). "Effect of Forest Bathing Trips on Human Immune Function." Nippon Medical School. *Environ Health Prev Med*. 2010 Jan; 15(1):9-17. doi: 10.1007/s12199-008-0068-3

[6] Li Q, Kobayashi M, Kumeda S, Ochiai T, Miura T, Kagawa T, Imai M, Wang Z, Otsuka T, Kawada T. 2016. "Effects of Forest Bathing on Cardiovascular and Metabolic Parameters in Middle-Aged Males." Evid Based Complement Alternat Me. 2016; 2016:2587381. doi: 10.1155/2016/2587381. Epub 2016 Jul 14.

[7] Mustonen, S., Tuorila, H. (2010). "Sensory Education Decreases Food Neophobia Score and Encourages Trying Unfamiliar Foods in 8 to12-year-old Children." *Food Quality and Preference*, volume 21, issue 4. June 2010. pages 353-360.

[8] Field, T. (2010). "Touch for Socioemotional and Physical Well-Being." *Elsevier Developmental Review*, Volume 30, Issue 4, December 2010. pages 367-383.

## Chapter 6

[1] Rudd,M., Vohs,K., Aaker, J. 2012. "Awe Expands People's Perception of Time and Enhances Well-Being." Stanford University and the University of Minnesota.

[2] McDonald, M., Wearing, S., Ponting, J. 2009. "The Nature of Peak Experience in Wilderness." *The Humanistic Psychologist*. 37. 370-385. 10.

[3] Ravizza, K. (1977). "Peak experiences in sport." *Journal of Humanistic Psychology*. 17. 35-40.

[4] Frederickson, L. and Anderson, D. (1999). "A Qualitative Exploration of the Wilderness Experience as a Source of Spiritual Inspiration." *Journal of Environmental Psychology*. 19. 21-39.

[5] J. Rubinstein, D. Meyer, J. Evans (2001). "Executive Control of Cognitive Processes in Task Switching." *Journal of Experimental Psychology: Human Perception and Performance*. 27 (4).

[6] A. C. Hafenbrack, Z. Kinias, S. G. Barsade. 2013. "Debiasing the Mind through Meditation: Mindfulness and the Sunk-Cost Bias". *Psychological Science*, 25 (2): 369 DOI: 10.1177/0956797613503853.

## Chapter 7

[1] Anderson, CL, Monroy, M, Keltner, D. 2018. "Awe in Nature Heals: Evidence from Military Veterans, At-Risk Youth, and College Students." Greater Good Science Center, University of California, Berkeley. Emotion. Dec;18(8):1195-1202. doi: 10.1037/emo0000442.

[2] Bai Y, Maruskin LA, Chen S, Gordon AM, Stellar JE, McNeil GD, Peng K, Keltner D. 2017. "Awe, the Diminished Self, and Collective Engagement: Universals and Cultural Variations in the Small Self." University of California, Berkeley, University of Toronto, University of

Tsinghua. J Pers Soc Psychol. Aug;113(2):185-209. doi: 10.1037/pspa0000087. Epub 2017 May 8.

[3] University of East Anglia. "It's Official— Spending Time Outside is Good for You." ScienceDaily.com, 6 July 2018. www.sciencedaily.com/ releases/2018/07/180706102842.htm.

[4] Repenski, Karen. "The Health Benefits of Some Sun Exposure." Consumer Reports.org, May 16, 2018. https://www.consumerreports.org/health-wellness/sun-cxposure-health-benefits/

[5] Loyola Press. "Canticle of the Sun." LoyolaPress.com, (Accessed April 18, 2020). https://www.loyolapress.com/ catholic-resources/prayer/traditional-catholic-prayers/ saints-prayers/canticle-of-the-sun-saint-francis-of-assisi/

[6] Emoto, Masaru. *The Hidden Messages in Water*, Atria Books, 2005.

[7] Piff PK, Dietze P, Feinberg M, Stancato DM, Keltner D. 2015. "Awe, the Small Self, and Prosocial Behavior." University of California, Irvine, New York University, University of Toronto, University of California, Berkeley. *J Pers Soc Psychol.* 2015 Jun;108(6):883-99. doi: 10.1037/ pspi0000018. PMID: 25984788.

[8] Suttie, Jill. "Why Trees Can Make You Happier." Greater Good Science Center, University of California, Berkeley. April 26, 2019. https://greatergood.berkeley. edu/article/item/why_trees_can_make_you_happier

## Chapter 8

[1] Mayo Clinic staff. "Positive Thinking: Stop Negative Self-Talk to Reduce Stress." Mayo Clinic, February 18, 2017. https://www.mayoclinic.org/healthy-lifestyle/ stress-management/in-depth/positive-thinking/art-20043950.

[2] Rauh, Sherry. "10 Surprising Health Benefits of Love." WebMD.com. January 30, 2009. https://www.webmd.com/sex-relationships/features/health-benefits#1

[3] Braud, William. "Experiencing Tears of Wonder-Joy: Seeing with the Heart's Eye." *Journal of Transpersonal Psychology* 33, no. 2. 2001: 99-112.

[4] Allen, Summer. "Eight Reasons Why Awe Makes Your Life Better." Greater Good Science Center, University of California, Berkeley, September 26, 2018. https://greatergood.berkeley.edu/article/item/eight_reasons_why_awe_makes_your_life_better.

[5] Mead, Elaine. "6 Benefits of Happiness, According to the Research." Positive Psychology.com, June 30, 2019. https://positivepsychology.com/benefits-of-happiness/.

[6] Mayo Clinic staff. "Stress Relief from Laughter? It's No Joke." Mayo Clinic, April 5, 2019. https://www.mayoclinic.org/healthy-lifestyle/stress-management/in-depth/stress-relief/art-20044456.

[7] Lindsey, Jessica. "How a Little Humor Can Improve Your Work Life." Greater Good Science Center, University of California, Berkeley, October 15, 2019. https://greatergood.berkeley.edu/article/item/how_a_little_humor_can_improve_your_work_life.

[8] Masci, David and Lipka, Michael. "Americans May be Getting Less Religious, but Feelings of Spirituality are on the Rise." Pew Research Center, January 21, 2016. https://www.pewresearch.org/fact-tank/2016/01/21/americans-spirituality/.

[9] Ibid.

[10] Newman, Kira. "Four Reasons to Cultivate Patience." Greater Good Science Center, University of California, Berkeley, April 4, 2016. https://greatergood.berkeley.edu/article/item/four_reasons_to_cultivate_patience

## Chapter 9

[1] Random Acts of Kindness Foundation. "Did you Know There are Scientifically Proven Benefits of being Kind?" Random Acts of Kindness.org, 2019. https://www.randomactsofkindness.org/the-science-of-kindness

[2] Piff, Paul, Dietze, Pia, Feinberg, Matthew, Stancato, Daniel, and Keltner, Dacher. "Awe, the Small Self, and Prosocial Behavior." University of California, Irvine, New York University, University of Toronto, and University of California, Berkeley. Journal of Personality and Social Psychology. 2015, Vol. 108, No. 6, 883– 899. http://dx.doi.org/10.1037/pspi0000018

[3] Mann, Mirele. "7 Scientific Facts about the Benefit of Doing Good." Goodnet.org, January 26, 2017. https://www.goodnet.org/articles/7-scientific-facts-about-benefit-doing-good

[4] Newberg, Andrew, Thomas Jefferson University Hospital. "The Spiritual Brain: Science and Religious Experience." The Great Courses, The Teaching Company, 2012. https://guidebookstgc.snagfilms.com/1682%20Spiritual%20Brain.pdf

[5] Piff, Paul, Dietze, Pia, Feinberg, Matthew, Stancato, Daniel, and Keltner, Dacher. "Awe, the Small Self, and Prosocial Behavior." University of California, Irvine, New York University, University of Toronto, and University of California, Berkeley. Journal of Personality and Social Psychology. 2015, Vol. 108, No. 6, 883– 899. http://dx.doi.org/10.1037/pspi0000018

[6] Amati, V., Meggiolaro, S., Rivellini, G., and Zaccarin, S. (2018) "Social Relations and Life Satisfaction: The Role of Friends." Genius, Volume 74, Issue 1, Page 7. DOI: 10.1186/s41118-018-0032-z, Published online at https://www.ncbi.nlm.nih.gov/pmc/articles/PMC5937874/

[7] Zhao, H., Zhang, H., Xu, Y., He, W., and Lu, J. 2019. "Why Are People High in Dispositional Awe Happier? The Roles of Meaning in Life and Materialism." *Frontiers in psychology*, *10*, 1208. doi:10.3389/fpsyg.2019.01208 Published online at: https://www.ncbi.nlm.nih.gov/pmc/articles/PMC6540826/#B59

[8] Marques, J. (2013). "Understanding the Strength of Gentleness: Soft-Skilled Leadership on the Rise." Journal of Business Ethics, Vol. 116, DOI: 10.1007/s10551-012-1471-7, Published online at https://www.researchgate.net/publication/257541882_Understanding_the_Strength_of_Gentleness_Soft-Skilled_Leadership_on_the_Rise

[9] Holman, David. "How Gentleness at Work Can Promote High-Quality Professional Care." Personnel Today.com, May 4, 2018. https://www.personneltoday.com/hr/how-gentleness-at-work-can-promote-high-quality-professional-care/

[10] Lonczak, Heather. "40+ Benefits of Self-Control and Self-Discipline." PositivePsychology.com, October 25, 2019. https://positivepsychology.com/benefits-self-control-discipline/

[11] Li, J., Li, A., Sun, Y., Li, H., Liu, L., Zhan, Y., Fan, W., and Zhong, Y. (2019). "The Effect of Preceding Self-Control on Prosocial Behaviors: The Moderating Role of Awe." Frontiers in Psychology, Volume: 10, Page: 682, DOI: https://doi.org/10.3389/fpsyg.2019.00682, Published online at https://www.frontiersin.org/articles/10.3389/fpsyg.2019.00682/full

[12] Friese, M., Schweizer, L., Arnoux, A., Sutter, F., and Wänke, M. (2014). "Personal prayer counteracts self-control depletion." *Conscious Cogn.* 29, 90–95. DOI: 10.1016/j.concog.2014.08.016,

Published online at https://www.ncbi.nlm.nih.gov/ pubmed?Db=pubmed&Cmd=ShowDetailView&Term ToSearch=22309814

**Chapter 10**

Kashdan, Todd., Stiksma, Melissa, Disabato, David, McKnight, David, Bekier, John, Kaji, Joel, and Lazarus, Rachel. "The Five-Dimensional Curiosity Scale Revised (5DCR)." George Mason University, Time, Inc., and Marketing and Research Resources, Inc. (2019)

[2] Ibid.

[3] Ibid.

[4] Cooper, Helene, Blumental, Ralphl, and Kean, Leslie, "Glowing Auras and 'Black Money': The Pentagon's Mysterious UFO Program," *The New York Times*, December 16, 2017.

[5] Watson, Stephanie. "How Crop Circles Work." HowStuffWorks.com, Accessed April 18, 2020. https://science.howstuffworks.com/science-vs-myth/ unexplained-phenomena/crop-circle6.htm

[6] Vigay, Paul. "Crop Circle Research." CropCircleResearch.com. Accessed April 18, 2020. https://www.cropcircleresearch.com/

[7] Ibid.

[8] Ibid.

[9] Szolosi, Andrew, Watson, Jason, and Ruddell, Edward. *The Benefits of Mystery in Nature on Attention: Assessing the impacts of presentation duration.* 2014. Frontiers in Psychology. 5: 1360.

**Chapter 11**

McPhetres, J. 2019. "Oh, the Things You Don't Know: Awe Promotes Awareness of Knowledge Gaps and Science

Interest." Cognition and Emotion, 33:8, 1599-1615, DOI: 10.1080/02699931.2019.1585331.

[2] Nelson-Coffey, S., Ruberton, P., Chancellor, J., Cornick, J., Blascovich, J., Lyubomirsky, S. (2019) The Proximal Experience of Awe. PLOS ONE 14(5): e0216780. DOI: 10.1371/journal.pone.0216780.

[3] Valdesolo, P. and Graham, J. 2014. "Awe, Uncertainty, and Agency Detection." *Psychological Science*, Vol. 25(1) 170-178, DOI: 10.1177/0956797613501884.

[4] Rudd, M., Hildebrand, C., and Vohs, K. 2018. "Inspired to Create: Awe Enhances Openness to Learning and the Desire for Experiential Creation." *Journal of Marketing Research*, Volume: 55 issue: 5, page(s): 766-781, DOI: https://doi.org/10.1177/0022243718802853.

## Chapter 12

Springer, Alex. "Who Experiences the Most Awe?" Greater Good Science Center, University of California, Berkeley, May 24, 2017. https://greatergood.berkeley.edu/article/item/who_experiences_the_most_awe.

[2] Weinstock, Cheryl. "How Church May Boost Mental Health." AARP, September 9, 2019. https://www.aarp.org/health/healthy-living/info-2019/religion-and-mental-health.html.

[3] Patterson, Jim. "Worship is Good for Your Health: Vanderbilt Study." Vanderbilt University, May 31, 2017. https://news.vanderbilt.edu/2017/05/31/worship-is-good-for-your-health-vanderbilt-study/.

[4] Büssing, A., Wirth, A. G., Reiser, F., Zahn, A., Humbroich, K., Gerbershagen, K., Schimrigk, S., Haupts, M., Hvidt, N. C., & Baumann, K. (2014). "Experience of Gratitude, Awe and Beauty in Life among Patients with Multiple Sclerosis and Psychiatric Disorders."

*Health and Quality of Life Outcomes*, 12, 63. https://doi.org/10.1186/1477-7525-12-63.

[5] Emmons, Robert. "Why Gratitude is Good." Greater Good Science Center, University of California, Berkeley, November 26, 2010. https://greatergood.berkeley.edu/article/item/why_gratitude_is_good.

[6] Happier Human staff. "31 Benefits of Gratitude: The Ultimate Science-Backed Guide." HappierHuman.com., February 27, 2020. https://www.happierhuman.com/benefits-of-gratitude/.

7 Boggio, P., Giglio, A., Nakao, C., Wingenbach, T., Marques, L., Koller, S., and Gruber, J. (2019). "Writing about Gratitude Increases Emotion-Regulation Efficacy." *The Journal of Positive Psychology*, DOI: 10.1080/17439760.2019.1651893.

[8] Newberg, Andrew, M.D. and Waldman, Mark Robert. *How God Changes Your Brain: Breakthrough Findings from a Leading Neuroscientist*. New York: Ballantine Books, 2009.

[9] Jilani, Zaid. "Can A Sense of Awe Improve Our Arguments?" Greater Good Science Center, University of California, Berkeley, December 2, 2019. https://greatergood.berkeley.edu/article/item/can_awe_improve_arguments.

Milton Keynes UK
Ingram Content Group UK Ltd.
UKHW020024141223
434291UK00015B/924